Liberating God

What the Church Doesn't Teach About the Bible

Donald Strickland

D1495355

TITLE: Liberating God: What the Church Doesn't Teach About the Bible

By: Donald Strickland

Edited by: 846 Publishing Company

Copyright 2022

and express written permission of the author with the exception of brief cited quotes. Thank you for respecting property rights.

Permission: For information on getting permission for reprints and excerpts, or to contact the author with your questions and/or comments, email revdonstrickland@gmail.com.

For

Gus and Ali.

You are the reason I

want the world to be a better place.

For my mother, who has lived courageously a life of hope in the midst of despair.

Thank you, Laura, for being my partner on the journey.

Thank you, Angee and John, for being critical lovers of Christianity and for all the hours of labor to make this project a reality.

TABLE OF CONTENTS

INTRODUCTION

Good News of Liberation for a Dysfunctional World

Abandoned at the doorstep of a brothel when she was only three months old, my mother's most formative years unfolded in a whorehouse in Mississippi.1 Being raped in a field is one of her earliest childhood memories. As a fifteen-year-old bride in what was tantamount to a shotgun wedding, the abuses she suffered offer glimpses into the trauma that served as preparation for raising her own eight children, of whom I am the youngest. Into such stories of heartbreak, abuse, and oppression, the gospel is spoken that God is a liberating God.

My mother would, from time to time, pack whatever she could into a few suitcases and make her own exodus. Each of her attempted escapes from her personal pharaoh inevitably set off a chain of events. With her gone, my drunk father would walk around the house with a loaded pistol,

---

[1] Stories are included with my mother's blessings. My father is deceased at the time of this writing.

threatening to kill himself. I still have one of the suicide notes he wrote, addressed specifically to me. On one particularly terrifying occasion, I remember lying in bed stiff as a board, hoping to make myself invisible as my father paced the hallway in the dead of night. I could see him through the cracked door of the bedroom that I shared with multiple siblings.

For hours, he paced back and forth, back and forth, his drunk-mumbling occasionally finding clarity: "I can't take this anymore. I *won't* take this anymore!" I laid there for what felt like an eternity, every muscle tensed, too terrified that any sound or movement would remind him of my presence on the other side of the door. Just ten years old, I wondered if he would merely kill himself, or if he would kill us kids first. Nights like those were long and still burn in my memory.

As an ordained minister, I often had difficulty preaching the gospel. Perhaps because I have been so blessed in my adult life, I found it increasingly impossible to pretend Jesus' gospel message of liberating the poor and oppressed (explicitly stated in Luke 4:18) was directed to me or the congregation I served. As an adult, I identified more with Israel after they reached the land of milk and honey. In the nation's youth, they were recipients of God's good news of liberation. "Let my people go!" Later in Israel's life, however, God's word spoken through the prophets was filled with warning and judgment. Something happened between the time of Israel's young life of abuses and its adult life as a rich nation overflowing with abundance. And it was undeniable that, as a pastor, I stood in a congregation of First World abundance; not among the poor and oppressed.

In the gospel stories, the Roman Empire was at odds with the Kingdom (or Rule) of God that Jesus inaugurated.[2] In a strange twist of history, however, it was the Roman elites who organized the church. And they organized it the same way they organized their empire, only instead of emperors and prefects and governors church leaders were called popes and bishops and priests. Emperor Constantine is remembered for going into battle with the emblem of Christ's cross on his soldier's shields. The same violent Empire that oversaw the crucifixion of Christ organized the church that bears his name. From its very beginnings, the church embodied the tension between a nonviolent Jesus who was crucified for sedition[3] and an Empire that murdered him.

---

[2] See Matthew 3:2, Mark 1:15, and Luke 4:18. The synoptic gospel are all clear that the "good news" (synonymous with "gospel," since both are English translations of the same Greek word, εὐαγγέλιον) is that God's rule has begun. The good news or gospel message is that God's rule has been inaugurated in the person and ministry of Jesus Christ.

[3] See John 19:19. The criminal offense displayed atop the cross as INRI (Iēsus Nazarēnus, Rēx Iūdaeōrum), which translates "Jesus of Nazareth, King of the Jews."

Though millennia have passed, nothing has changed. Most First World churches are oblivious to just how much they have in common with the Roman Empire that was at odds with God's Kingdom. They are oblivious to how much their church leaders have in common with the religious elites (the Pharisees and Sadducees in the Bible, for instance) that helped perpetuate the Empire's rule over the occupied Jews while helping kill Jesus.

Religious leaders have taught churchgoers to identify with the occupied, Jewish peasants with whom Jesus journeyed and to whom Jesus ministered. How can First World churches proclaim any truth so long as they pretend that they have more in common with occupied peasants than with those who benefit most from Empire?

Of course, the message had to be changed. The church of Empire cannot promote a Jesus whose primary message is divine sedition in favor of God's rule. For instance, Empire can't meaningfully tell the story of a pregnant Mary fleeing the country as a political refugee for her part in the seditious plot. The break is so complete that most churches have an unwritten doctrine that religion and politics should never go together. And the state plays right along by granting a non-taxed status so long as the church doesn't get political – a contemporary example of the Empire telling the church how to organize itself.

The church's capacity for voluntary amnesia has led to what is now the most popular forms of so-called Christianity. Christians have become obsessed with two narcissistic, dangerous ideas: (1) how to get rich (aka "the prosperity gospel") and (2) how to live forever (aka "eternal life in Heaven after death"). How have these two religious goals become the most popular interpretations of the gospel, particularly when Christ preached *against* storing up treasures on earth and *in favor of* taking up your cross and risking even dying in his service?

If what you just read offends you, I understand. There was a time it offended me as well. In fact, it offends so many churchgoers who learn that church leadership has not been completely forthcoming, that one writer (Paul Ricoeur) gave the offense a name. He called it a time of "desert wanderings." What he meant is that learning the truth can often leave us feeling disillusioned and angry, as if we are wandering in the desert. Christians who have faithfully attended church and Sunday School have been spoon-fed a fantastic (if narcissistic) fairy tale. Uncritically believing what the church taught us when we were children is what Ricoeur called the "first naivete." When that fairy tale is shattered, it is painful to accept. But it is only then that true learning and discipleship can occur.

In the coming pages, I will present a different perspective on God and what God is up to in the world. But know this before you turn another page; what is written here may not be easy to read and may be even harder to accept. If you approach these pages with your preconceived ideas about the gospel, you will, understandably, dismiss what I share as misguided, wrong, or worse, heresy. If that is the conclusion you draw, so be it. But, for the remainder of the book, I challenge you to set aside what you think you know about God and the bible and entertain the possibility that most Christians have not been told the whole truth.

The most brilliant minds in science once believed the earth was flat and that the sun revolved around the earth. Pharmacists sold soda as a miracle drug at their counters. Trans fats were once recommended on the Food Pyramid. Today, they are banned in the U. S. The point is that we often make mistakes in our understanding despite our knowledge and education. So, I challenge you to lay down your assumptions, just for a time. Don't worry, they will be there waiting for you when you finish reading. You can simply pick them all back up again, if you wish. But I suspect you will, instead, learn something so magnificent about the God that anointed Jesus that you choose to leave them behind.

To more fully understand the following, you will need to entertain five premises:

First, we have been taught a doctrine of salvation that encourages us to be saved *from*. Many Christians have been taught to rejoice over being saved *from* sin, *from* death, and, of course, from the fiery pits of Hell. What I will ask you to consider is that you are also saved *for*. In salvation, we are saved *for* God's rule. This is the overwhelming theme of this work, and will be discussed in the chapters to come. God's claim upon us includes a salvation that comes with responsibility for one another. Without clarity about what we are saved *for*, we may become party to the narcissistic religions masquerading as so-called Christianity today.

Second, you must contemplate who "the rich" are that Jesus so frequently refers to. If you are seeking to identify "the rich" by looking outward, pointing at millionaires and billionaires, demanding that they alter their ways and share with the poor and middle class, you will miss the important point that you may be among "the rich" whom Jesus called to follow him.

Third, consider the possibility that the great communion is not that which takes place on Sunday morning when we pass stale wafers and flavorless juice or cheap wine. Instead, Christ calls us to a Love Feast which looks far different than our ritual. Most notably, it would include "the least of these." Therefore, if you look left and right during your church's communion practice and don't see the homeless, hungry, lonely, and desperate, then what you're doing is not biblical communion.

Perhaps the most difficult concept you will face as you read on is the idea that the Bible was never meant to be the fourth person of the Trinity. The Bible is not a book to be worshipped. It is a sacred book, which means we Christians set it aside for a special purpose. It is powerful, instructive, and an inspired anthology, but Christians must reconcile the fact that there are deep divisions among biblical writers if they want to truly understand what is written in its pages. Otherwise, readers of the Bible will inevitably confuse difference and division with contradiction:

- Does the Bible want us to believe, as Moses wrote, that you reap what you sow? What then do we do with sinless Job who suffered through no fault of his own?

- Does the Bible want us to believe, with Isaiah, that the wicked are punished? What then do we do with the biblical law that a woman who is raped must marry her rapist?

- Does the Bible want us to believe that Peter is the Rock upon whose spoken truth the church is built? What then do we do with the fact that the Apostle Paul called Peter a hypocrite who misunderstood the gospel?

- Does the Bible want women silenced in the church as Paul supposedly taught? What then do we do with the women that the same Paul put in positions of church leadership or prophetic leaders like Deborah who were called to proclaim God's word?

- Is God the one who demands murderous battle in the Bible, genocidally insisting that every living thing is slaughtered? Or is God the voice of love and peace?

All of these issues and more are addressed in the pages that follow. When we face these apparent inconsistencies in scripture, we look to explain them away rather than embrace the tension they create. Perhaps the most challenging of all ideas in this book is this: *the only reason we struggle with so-called contradictory voices in the Bible is because we've been taught to read the Bible wrongly.*

The only way to truly understand the *Christ*-ian scriptures is to understand Christ to be the living, breathing, and speaking Word of God. Remember, John never said "In the beginning was the word and the word was with God, and the word was the **bible**." John said the word is Christ.[4] He is the

---

[4] See John 1:14

Word made flesh who dwelled, lived, and walked among us. Until that point becomes clear, the study of the Bible cannot rightly begin.

A childhood marked by suffering at the hands of my personal Pharoah shaped the way I heard and understood the gospel. I was under no delusions about God sparing me from every evil thing. What I gained from my adversity, instead, was the experience of Christ as truly Emmanuel — God with us in suffering, God with us in pain, God with us in brokenness. The biblical gospel is the good news that God's rule is among us and is the salvation of all of creation. In both Old Testament and New, that is the gospel, and it permeates all of scripture.

The Most Important Word in the Bible that Christians Don't Know

Jubilee may be the most important word that most Christians do not know. Perhaps more than any other word in the Bible, *Jubilee* captures the message of Jesus in particular and the scriptures in general. It was a foundational principle given by God to the chosen people. Carried down from the same mountaintop as the Ten Commandments, and just as critical to understanding what God was doing in the world, Jubilee embodies the vision of justice proclaimed by all the prophets on behalf of families who suffered the brutality of poverty.

Simply put, Jubilee is God's specific plan for liberation. Every seven years, and again every fiftieth year, was to be a Jubilee Year. Through a massive redistribution of wealth and power, slaves were to be set free. Crushing debt was to be forgiven. Family land was to be returned to those who had lost it. Brutal social and economic conditions that nurtured inequality and left people languishing without the means to provide for themselves or their families were to be wiped away in one fell swoop. Again, Jubilee was God's specific plan for liberation.

Throughout scripture, especially among the prophets, the concept of Jubilee expanded and took on new forms. The vision of godly rule eventually included salvation from oppression in all its forms, including dysfunctional family systems, death-dealing political realities, crushing economic conditions, and even toxic religion. Originating in a small band of freed Egyptian slaves, all of creation would eventually be included in the promise of God's plan for liberation.

Jubilee is not an insignificant footnote in the Bible. Rather, it is the entire plot. The story of scripture, throughout, is that God is saving the world from sin, death, and the devil; and God's specific plan for salvation is Jubilee. The biblical vision of God's rule means the end of not only discrimination based on race, gender, sexuality, physical ability, religion, ethnicity, or nationality. It means the end of injustice in *all* its forms, including those hidden in the family secrets and private lives of its victims. Salvation is life under God's rule. The gospel message is for all who live with the consequences of evil. The Bible relates the cosmic struggle for justice.

In a world in which injustice is no respecter of persons, Jubilee is a dangerous hope. Scripture does not hide the fact that challenging systems of oppression can be deadly. Mary, the mother of Jesus, became a political refugee for her participation in the *coup d'état* against the king.[5]

---

[5] See Matthew 13ff.

John the baptizer was beheaded for his public criticism of Herod.[6] The gospel does not pretend that discipleship is safe. In fact, observing and promoting Jubilee is precisely what got Jesus killed, much the same as it killed Carole Denise, Addie May Collins, Carole Robertson, and Cynthia Wesley. These young victims of the 16th Street Baptist Church Bombing died while participating in the pursuit of God's justice. As Civil Rights organizations like the *Southern Christian Leadership Conference* and the *Congress on Racial Equality* were meeting at the 16th Street Baptist Church to organize and train young nonviolent marchers to protest and fill up the city jail, Klansmen were planting bombs beneath the steps of the church.

Stories like my mother's are powerful because they capture what Civil Rights organizers knew. Stories have the power to expose the forces of evil that perpetuate poverty and inequity. Images of people of color being brutalized by police dogs and firehoses were stomach-turning. But they were also the power to change the world. By refusing to keep their stories hidden, and, instead, putting them on public display, evil could no longer hide in shadowy places. By telling stories of abuse through protests, marches, and sit-ins the, then, common, every day, ordinary acts of violence against people

---

[6] See Luke 3:19.

of color were turned into acts of resistance. Our stories contain power to change the world.

The Jubilee gospel insists that God has a heart for every person that the world deems disposable. Things that we imagine make us unworthy of love and respect in *this* world are the very things that make us worthy of the gospel. We may be inclined to tuck away stories that reveal too much brokenness, weakness, or pain. We want to give the impression that we have it all together despite the truth of our inner and outer battles. But, as scripture reveals, being *normal* does not mean having it all together. The Bible does not allow us to get away with such myths. In fact, our most sacred stories reveal that being *abnormal* is the most normal thing of all.

The Bible Tells the Truth about Family

The Bible has an uncanny way of telling the truth about what it means to be "family." In the very first chapter of the Bible there is a story about Adam and Eve, the first family ever. Almost immediately that very first family is embroiled in deception. Hiding from God is one of the very first human acts. Then the first time in history that a family finds itself in trouble, the first husband blames all of his misery on his wife.[7] Turn the page and that first couple have children, Cain and Abel. The very first sibling murders his brother.[8] And, so, the story of family begins. From the very beginning, according to scripture, to be a "normal" family is to be a broken family.

It is no exaggeration to say that just about every family since Adam and Eve's has had its share of turmoil and heartbreak.

- The ark builder, Noah, got so angry with his son, Ham, that he cursed him (Genesis 9:25). There's no record that they ever spoke to one another again.

---

[7] Genesis 3:12

[8] Genesis 4:8.

- Father of nations, Abraham, permanently banished his oldest son, Ishmael (Genesis 21:14).

- Jacob's mom put wool on his arms to make them appear hairy like his older brother (Genesis 27:16) in order to trick her blind and dying husband. She wanted to ensure that her favorite son got the family inheritance instead of Dad's favorite son.

- His own brothers sold Joseph into slavery and then dipped his coat of many colors in goat's blood to convince their dad his son was dead (Genesis 37:18ff).

- King David's son, Amnon, forcibly raped his own sister, Tamar (2 Samuel 13:14).

The frightful tales go on and on. The Bible is riddled with example after example of broken, *real* families. Even Jesus' own family was publicly saying that he was, "out of his mind."[9] Mom and brothers and sisters all went out to restrain Jesus; and they told anyone who would listen, "Don't pay any attention to him. He's lost his senses." To hear

---

[9] Mark 3:21.

Mark tell it, Jesus' family was not the best example of a support structure. And why would they be? Biblical families are much like every other family—like mine, like yours.

Disagreement and Division

Dysfunction, however, is not limited to blood relatives in the Bible. The fictive kinship of "God's people" also reveals just how normal divisiveness really is. Since the great biblical families like Abraham and Noah and King David were marked by enmity and deep division, maybe it should not surprise us that other great names of the Bible suffered the same "normal."

There is a difference, however, between disagreement and division. There are four separate accounts of Jesus' ministry, for instance, and each account is different. Who visited the tomb on resurrection Sunday varies by gospel. John recounts only Mary Magdalene, while Luke remembers Mary Magdalene, Joanna, James' mother Mary, and "other women." Mark adds Salome and omits Joanna, while Matthew speaks of only "Mary Magdalene and the other Mary."

Examples of differences abound in the gospels, mostly for theological reasons. For instance, whereas in Matthew, Mark, and Luke, Jesus *ate* the Passover with the disciples, in John, Jesus *was* the Passover lamb. In other words, John had a particular theological reason for placing the Passover meal after Jesus' crucifixion.

Early in the second century CE, the four gospels were edited into one. In an effort to eliminate differences and do away with seeming contradiction, a man named Tatian combined all the gospels together and called his new unified account the *Diatessaron*. No longer would the church be forced to wrestle with different versions of the Jesus story.

With great wisdom, however, the church rejected Tatian's unified gospel. The differences, the church insisted, add to the richness of our sacred texts. They add to a fuller understanding of the God made known in Jesus Christ. They tell a larger story than a single voice could ever do. The church believed that eliminating differences would only make the gospel more difficult to understand.

The impulse to smooth over differences remains powerful in the church. The popular Christmas nativity scene with wise men and shepherds all together at the manger is a consolidation of the different accounts from Matthew and Luke. Division, however, is different than disagreement. Unlike difference, which adds to the richness of biblical accounts, division may make reading the Bible more confusing.

Moses and Job are powerful examples of the kind of division readers can expect to find in the Bible. Division is not merely differing accounts of what happened. Division is differing accounts of who God is and what God is up to in the world.

Moses[10] insisted that those who do evil will be cursed *in this life*, living a life filled with "disaster, panic, and frustrations in everything you attempt to do, until you are destroyed and perish quickly, on account of the evil of your deeds."[11] The righteous, on the other hand, can expect blessings "in all they undertake." They will "abound in prosperity."[12]

Job is one of the harshest critics of Moses' dangerous "you reap what you sow" theology. Contrary to what the Torah says, Job insisted, neither the righteous nor the sinner get what they deserve in this life. In their suffering at the hands of the wicked who steal and kill, the poor and destitute cry out for God's help, "yet God pays no attention."[13] "[T]he wicked live on, reach old age, and grow mighty in power . . . [T]hey spend their days in prosperity and go to the grave in peace."[14]

---

[10] While tradition held that Moses wrote the first five books of the Bible, scholarship has since shown that authorship is much more complex. For more information on why scholars believe Moses did *not* write the first five books of the Bible, see Richard Friedman's *Who Wrote the Bible* (New York: Simon and Schuster, 2019).

[11] Deuteronomy 28:16–46.

[12] Deuteronomy 28:1–15.

[13] Job 24:12.

[14] Job 21:7, 13.

Recognizing division among its authors is one of the most important interpretive keys to understanding the Bible.

Some ideas in the Bible are just bad![15] While walking with his disciples, they came across a blind man and asked, "Jesus, who sinned, this man or his parents that he was born blind?" The disciples' way of thinking about God was grounded in the biblical notion that you reap what you sow. Jesus, however, refused to blame the blind man for his blindness. "Neither this man nor his parents sinned." Healing the blind man was dangerous because it challenged the long-established tradition of blaming the victim instead of helping the victim. That is a bad idea! Far from trivial, such blame-the-victim theology makes the difference between treating suffering as God's punishment and treating it as the object of divine liberation. Readers most resistant to the claim that some ideas in the Bible are just bad are the same readers unwilling to suspend the doctrine that the Bible is the infallible Word of God. As already claimed, that title belongs only to Jesus Christ. He, alone, is the Word of God. And just like believers today have different ideas about God, so did believers during the fifteen hundred years or so in which the Bible was written.

---

[15] See Deuteronomy 22:29, 29. In these verses, a victim of rape is required to marry their rapist.

The Pharisees and Jesus were also divided over what God was up to in the world. Over and over again the gospels recount the stories of Jesus being challenged by the priestly class. So divided were the Pharisees and Jesus that the priests plotted his murder.16 Pharisees and Jesus were deeply divided over what it meant to be the people of God.

This dysfunction among the followers of Yahweh was not limited to Jesus and the priestly class, however. Paul and Peter also experienced divisions so significant that they never reconciled. Both the Acts of the Apostles and Paul's letter to the Galatians speak of the Antioch incident, as it is called. Since Galatians was written by Paul, it provides a first-hand account.

In Galatians 2, using the same language that Jesus reserved for the Pharisees, Paul calls the Apostle Peter a hypocrite. The same Peter-the-rock upon whom Jesus would build his church disagreed significantly with the Apostle Paul concerning what God's work in the world looked like.

Peter (among others) went back on his word and insisted that Gentile converts had to be circumcised. Paul saw this as a rejection of the gospel. Peter and "the circumcision faction," Paul insisted, had completely misunderstood the character of God. God's work in the world has

---

16 John 11:53.

nothing to do with foreskin, Paul insisted. Infuriated, he wrote, *I wish the circumcision faction would follow their own advice to the extreme and castrate themselves!*[17] Paul's break with Peter was complete! As far as scripture recounts, Paul and Peter never saw eye to eye. Their understanding of what God was doing in the world became an enduring reason for enmity between them.

The church has come to expect division and enmity between the good-guy-Jesus and the bad-guy-Pharisees. But the division between Moses and Job or Peter and Paul may be completely unexpected. So many of us have wrongly been taught that the Bible is a collection of writers who essentially agree about the character of God. The deeper we look, the easier it is to recognize that teaching as misguided. Contrary to the attitude of many Christians, the Bible is not the fourth person of the Trinity. It is not an object of worship. Rather, it is our sacred record of God's people; a people who were as divided then as God's people are today. Biblical writers were often no better at seeing eye to eye than were the biblical families whose stories we hold in such high esteem.

There are many modern day Tatians who work hard at smoothing over difference and division while trying to prove that all the biblical writers were in

---

[17] Galatians 5:12.

agreement. They deny the gospels give varying accounts. They smooth over critical theological divisions between the apostles. They deny the reality that there are varied understandings of God throughout the Bible.

Yet doing so creates a barrier to understanding. By forcing agreement where it does not exist, the gospel message becomes unintelligible. God can be said to be Love[18] in one moment, and a committer of genocide in the next.[19] The God who in one breath proclaims, "Let the children come to me"[20] in the next demands people to "dash the babies' heads against the rocks."[21] The God-of-forced-agreement cannot help but be as bipolar as one voice demanding that "You will hunt down your enemies [and] kill them with the sword,"[22] and then commanding you to "Love your enemies, and pray for those who persecute you."[23] The greatest obstacle to understanding the Bible comes from the mistaken assumption that all biblical writers were of one accord. They were not! Like every other

---

[18] 1 John 4:7–21.

[19] Deuteronomy 20:16.

[20] Matthew 19:14.

[21] Psalm 137:9.

[22] Leviticus 26:7.

[23] Matthew 5:44.

biblical family that is embroiled in division, biblical authors did not always see eye to eye.

God of Old and New Testaments

Far from an "Old Testament" that merely recounts a vindictive and violent God, the varied voices in the Hebrew Bible illuminate the gospel with surprising contrast and clarity. Though no longer in existence today, Marcion, during the second century CE, founded a church that claimed that the Old Testament God was a different God than the New Testament God. Marcion has no contemporary disciples, but countless Christians still struggle to make sense of how different the God of the Old Testament is from the God of the New.

Much of the misunderstanding, however, is a result of how Christians have used the Old Testament over the millennia. In other words, Christians are mostly to blame for the misconception that the Old Testament God is a god of law, while the New Testament God is a god of love. Martin Luther, for instance, emphasized the Old Testament law in his Small Catechism, which he wrote to teach church members about the Bible. In fact, Luther reorganized the order of the Catholic catechism so that the section on law (and, consequently, the Old Testament) would appear before the section concerning gospel (or the New Testament). The way Luther saw it, the order of the Catechism should reflect the historical order of salvation. First came the Old Testament book of law, he taught. Then came the New Testament book of gospel.

It is no surprise, then, that children learning about the nature of scripture, law, and gospel would imagine the Old Testament as primarily a book of laws and the New Testament as a book of gospel. Nothing could be further from the truth.

To the surprise of many Christians, Jesus taught nothing new. Every bit of gospel that he proclaimed came directly from the Old Testament. *While the Pharisees emphasized the Sabbath Law that was brought down from Mount Sanai in Exodus 20:10, Jesus emphasized the gospel that Moses brought down from that same mountaintop in Leviticus 25.* While the Sadducees insisted that the law prohibited any work to be performed on the Sabbath, Jesus insisted that the Sabbath was all about work—namely, God's liberating *work* of Jubilee, which was itself a Sabbath of liberation from debt and slavery. Sadly, the reason most Christians imagine the Old Testament to be about a god who is angry and legalistic is because those are the voices the church chose to emphasize.

"Teacher, which is the greatest Commandment," asked an "expert in the law."[24] Jesus answered by citing two Old Testament passages, Deuteronomy 6:5 and Leviticus 19:18. The answer was to love, because love "sums up all the law and all the prophets."[25] If Jesus characterized the heart of the

---

[24] Matthew 22:35, 36.

[25] Matthew 22:40.

God of the Old Testament by referring to seemingly obscure Old Testament passages that are unfamiliar to most Christians, why does the church catechize youth into a belief that the Old Testament is summed up by the words "Thou shalt not"?

Most Christian teaching about the Old Testament is grounded in the doctrine of supersessionism. Supersessionism is the belief that Christianity has somehow defeated, superseded, or replaced Judaism. In fact, even the label "Old" in the title *Old* Testament is loaded with innuendo. The "Old" is somehow considered inferior to the "New," according to supersessionist claims.

The pages that follow, however, will show that the so-called "Old Testament" is filled with gospel proclamation. One of the first challenges in reading this book, then, will be to suspend approximately two thousand years of Christian teaching about the "Old" Testament, characterized by an angry, violent, and judgmental God. Instead, I invite you to see there the same God of the gospel that Jesus and other New Testament figures proclaimed.

To aid in that journey, the label "Old Testament" will no longer do. Of course, the label "Old" was not part of the original texts. It was added by the church centuries after Jesus' death and resurrection. Instead, the following pages will use the label "the

Hebrew Bible." In other words, we begin with the same scriptures that Jesus, himself, used to reveal the heart of God.

PART ONE: JUBILEE AND THE HEBREW BIBLE

Chapter 1: WHEN MOSES GAVE US THE GOSPEL

The Law at Mount Sinai

Sunday schools across America (and a particular Charlton Heston movie) would have us believe that the Ten Commandments were at the heart of Moses' message brought down from the mountaintop. Yet Moses did not just bring the law from atop Mount Sinai: he also brought down the gospel or good news that God is a liberating God.

One of my philosophy professors was fond of saying, "To see is not to see." To focus our vision on an object (or subject, in this case) is, inevitably, to permit so much more to go unnoticed—like the viral video that invites viewers to count how many times the players wearing white pass a basketball. After viewers have concentrated on each exchange of the ball, the narrator asks the surprising question, "Did you see the gorilla walk across the court?"[26] To see is not to see.

---

[26] See http://bit.do/selectiveattention.

Luther's emphasis on the Ten Commandments was, in part, a reflection of what he saw happening in the Church of his day. Concerned that the Church had lost its way, he sought effective ways to demonstrate the important difference between law and gospel.

Theology Professor Ed Schroeder referred to "the grammar of law" and the "grammar of gospel."[27] Law, he said, is fond of the verb *should*. The Ten Commandments serve as an effective example, especially with their emphasis on *Thou shalts* and *Thou shalt nots*. Always transactional, the law is fond of saying, "If you [human] do such and so, then I [God] will do such and so."[28] As Schroeder noted, "Even when the word 'Jesus' appears in such a sentence, the grammatical structure of 'If/Then' makes it law no matter what."

The gospel on the other hand uses verbs like *because* and *therefore*. "God is doing, [or] has done such and so in Christ, THEREFORE you now do this or that." This is the grammar of gospel.

---

[27] Ed Schroeder, *The Promise of Lutheran Ethics – Law/Gospel Grammar*, https://crossings.org/the-promise-of-lutheran-ethics-lawgospel-grammar/

[28] Ed Schroeder, *The Promise of Lutheran Ethics – Law/Gospel Grammar*, https://crossings.org/the-promise-of-lutheran-ethics-lawgospel-grammar/.

By understanding the distinction between the grammar of law and the grammar of gospel, it becomes easy to recognize gospel in the Old Testament. For instance, when God commands the care of freed slaves, widows, orphans, and strangers, God concludes, "Remember that you were a slave in the land of Egypt and the Lord your God redeemed you. *Therefore*, I am commanding you this today."[29] The command to care for others was not grounded in what one *should* do. It was grounded in what *God had already done*, which enabled God's people to do likewise.

Luther, however, did not make such a distinction. Some have insisted that Luther's own *clearly* drawn lines between "The New Testament [that] properly consists of promises and exhortations, [and] the Old Testament [that] consists of law and threats" were at odds with his recognition that the gospel was available to the Hebrews.[30] For instance, Luther noted that "the patriarchs, prophets, and devout kings in the Old Testament . . . received the Holy Spirit secretly on account of their faith in the coming Christ."[31] Some have tried

---

[29] See, for example, Deuteronomy 15:15 (English Standard Version) and Deuteronomy 24:22.

[30] See Professor of Ecclesiastical History at the University of Glasgow, Charlotte Methuen's *Luther and Calvin: Religious Revolutionaries*. Lion Books, 2011, page 71.

[31] See Volume 26, pages 203 to 211, of *The American Edition of Luther's Works*, Concordia Publishing House (June 24, 2007)

to show that Luther's distinction between the Hebrew and Christian scriptures was nuanced.

While well meaning, such arguments are difficult to find compelling. There is much stronger evidence that Luther, at times, drew almost Marcion-like distinctions between what he called the Old and New Testaments.[32] Perhaps Luther's own struggle with the legalists of his time, which he firmly believed were placing people's souls in bondage, motivated his emphasis on the *Law* of Moses, as well as the consequent lack of ability to see the *Gospel* that Moses proclaimed. In other words, Luther's emphasis on law was likely a reflection of his own context. He looked to scripture to provide a check against the abuses of the church that he loved. Understanding Luther's interpretation of the "Old Testament" as occasional rather than universal helps to explain his emphasis on drawing sharp distinctions between law and gospel.

"As soon as the coin in the coffers ring, the soul from purgatory springs" was a common refrain that typified the exploitation of ordinary Christians in Luther's day. The church collected tithes as indulgences that promised a reduced penalty for sinners, living or deceased. The church was capitalizing on people's fear that God would make

---

[32] See *Luther's Works*, vol. 35, ed. E. Theodore Bachmann (Philadelphia, PA: Muhlenberg Press, 1960), 235–26).

them suffer. St. Peter's Basilica was funded in large part on the fear that law and judgment afforded. Luther's life-giving response was to emphasize that grace defined our relationship with God, not law. Like Paul, Luther insisted that the power of the law to condemn was put to death on the cross of Christ.

For centuries, the Protestant church emphasized Moses' role as law giver, perpetuating Protestantism's failed capacity to see him as anything else. Far from a complex figure in Hebrew history, centuries of children (and adults) were taught about a one-dimensional Moses who freed the slaves and gave the law. To this day, the Protestant church that I love too often fails to teach about the Moses who proclaimed the very same gospel that Jesus proclaimed. In fact, this gospel is the single thread that weaves together the entirety of the scripture. From beginning to end, the gospel message is prominent and powerful.

The Gospel at Mount Sinai

Imagine for a moment that you have never heard the epic story of Exodus 22—the story of Moses going up the mountain to convene with God and returning with stone tablets on which were written the Ten Commandments. Imagine, instead, that you have only heard the story of Moses bringing down from the mountaintop the gospel of Jubilee. Jubilee was the celebration that took place among the Hebrews at the end of each seven-year and fifty-year span. Levitical law required that all slaves were to be freed at those times, all debts owed canceled, and all land returned to its original owners. Thus, every Jubilee was an event of divine grace. Imagine that all you knew of Moses was this practice of radical mercy and liberation.

Surprisingly, this, and not the Ten Commandments, characterizes almost every Old Testament Prophet's understanding of Moses' message from above. The Hebrew Bible is brimming with gospel proclamation. And that proclamation is just as easily identifiable in Exodus or Leviticus or Jeremiah as it is in the Gospels of Matthew or Mark or Luke.

The importance of the two paragraphs above cannot be overstated. The Hebrew Bible is filled with the very same gospel proclamation as the New Testament. In fact, to make his proclamation, Jesus utilized specific authors of the only sacred text he recognized: The Hebrew Bible.

Chapter 2: EXODUS AS JUBILEE

Making the Familiar Unfamiliar

Long before Moses led the slaves to freedom, a similar ancient story was already being shared. Sargon, son of Jochebed and Amran, was born into grave danger—so much so that his mother, in order to save his life from the powers-that-be who sought to kill him, placed him in a reed basket, sealed it with pitch, and sent him floating down the river to safety. Eventually, he was discovered by the gardener of the royal family and was raised as a son.

The story plot of Sargon is nearly identical to the one written of Moses in Exodus 2. Remembered as the very first figure in the Middle East to rule over an empire, Sargon the Great ruled hundreds of years before the story of Moses. No wonder most scholars agree that the tale of Moses' early childhood was modeled after that of the first Great Emperor.

But why? What reason would the writers of Moses' story have in borrowing so heavily from the legend of Sargon? Wouldn't everyone have been familiar with the story of the famous emperor? Wouldn't people immediately have recognized the story of Moses as a sort of fraud, as plagiarism, as a copycat tale?

Answering this question invites us to think about Bible stories as primarily theological. In other words, they are stories intended, first and foremost, to tell us not about Moses but about God. They prompt us to wonder: Who is *God*? What is *God* up to in the world?

If the stories in the Bible are first theological, then it makes sense that their writing could represent a variety of literary genres. In other words, there is no one literary genre best suited for God-talk. If the primary purpose is to talk about God, then every genre is up for grabs, from allegory (Psalm 80:8–12) to poetic drama (Judges 5:15b–18) to historical allusion through fable (Judges 9:8–15) to imagery and symbolism (Ecclesiastes 12:1–7) to parable (Matthew 13:1–23), and so on.

It may add to our difficulties in understanding the Bible if we insist that the biblical writers were historians first and theologians second. We might imagine that they were writing historical books rather than theological ones. Doing so, however, fails to take into account their literary genius. Biblical writers were fluent in many literary styles, not just historical reporting. And they used them liberally.[33]

If the story of Moses is first theological, then the answer to our question takes on different possibilities. What *theological* purpose might the writers have had in borrowing so heavily from the then well-known origin story of Sargon?

Sargon's story was the creation of "Empire" upon the earth. Moses' story was the undoing of "Empire" upon the earth. In the former, a king was born to rule over a people. In the latter, a king and his armies are swallowed up because they would not "let my people go."[34] The theological purpose of the story tells us much about the character of God the Hebrews worshiped.

It helps to remember that it was never part of God's plan that the people should have a king to rule over them. It was Israel, not God, who demanded a king. 1 Samuel 8:7 remembers God lamenting, "They have rejected me from being king over them."

What looks like a retelling of the story of Empire turns out to be a great reversal. Readers who first

---

[33] The demand that biblical literature be a sort of video-tapeable history is a product of the Enlightenment. Such concerns belong much more to our time than to biblical times. Ancient stories in both the oral and written tradition were told in a complex array of literary genres. The art of storytelling was full of complexity.

[34] Exodus 9:1.

would have thought, "We know how this story ends. All hail King Moses," would have been shocked at the unexpected turn of events.

What Is God Up To?

Perhaps the most powerful revelation that comes out of the Exodus story is the morality of God. Over and over again a divine law is given, followed by the refrain, "Remember that you were once a slave in the land of Egypt; therefore, I am commanding you to do this."[35]

The experience of being slaves for four hundred years shaped the moral compass of the Hebrews deeply. Complete with protected classes like the widow, the orphan, and the stranger, the treatment of those who were most vulnerable was non-negotiable. Treat them with kindness and generosity. Care for them. Protect them. "You shall not deprive a resident alien or an orphan of justice; you shall not take a widow's garment in pledge. Remember that you were a slave in Egypt and the Lord your God redeemed you from there; therefore, I command you to do this."[36]

This story of the end of Empire and the vulnerable-protecting laws that were born out of generational suffering[37] gives shape to the entire prophetic tradition. When Amos complained that the poor

---

[35] Deuteronomy 24:22.

[36] Deuteronomy 24:17, 18.

[37] The descendants of Jacob were slaves in Egypt for four hundred years, spanning many generations (Genesis 15:13).

were purchased with silver, and the needy for a pair of sandals, he was railing against an Empire that had forgotten its God.[38] Or, as Jeremiah wrote, "Thus says the Lord: Act with justice and righteousness and deliver from the hand of the oppressor anyone who has been robbed. And do no wrong or violence to the alien, the orphan, or the widow, or shed innocent blood."[39] Or as Isaiah put it, "Bringing offerings is futile; incense is an abomination... I cannot endure your [religious] assemblies... Your hands are full of blood... remove the evil of your doings... seek justice, rescue the oppressed, defend the orphan, plead for the widow."[40]

The Exodus story is so much more than the liberation of *one* band of slaves. It is a story that captures one of the most significant revelations of who God is and what God is up to in the world.

The point is not historical, as if the story were about a particular place and time when Moses was alive. The point is global. It is about all places and all times. God takes the side of the oppressed, the marginalized, the outcast, the downtrodden.

---

[38] Amos 8:6.

[39] Jeremiah 22:3.

[40] Isaiah 1:13ff.

This means, of course, that *"the chosen people" were not "chosen" because of their ethnicity. God is not a racist.* Rather, the chosen people were chosen because God is on the side of the oppressed, and the "chosen" were an enslaved people. The very creation of the nation of Israel was an event of Jubilee whose founding event was this act of letting the captives go free.

Chapter 3: JUBILEE JUSTICE IN DAVID AND GOLIATH

The Real Underdog

It is so obvious that it sounds silly to say, but in our day and time the use of power to oppress and subjugate those who are weaker is frowned upon. In a manner of speaking, those who are weak are afforded greater moral latitude than those who are strong. As a culture, we do not like bullies, and it is likely that this moral sentiment comes from the Bible. Just like the story of Jesus, who was an innocent victim of brutality, the divine morality found in the Exodus story takes the side of the victim, the weak, and the vulnerable.

In fact, American culture lives in the ironic tension of both coveting power while, at the same time, demonizing those who use their power to exploit and harm others. The conflagration of moral outrage concerning millionaire Hollywood moguls whose abuse of power sparked #metoo, or the unending images of unarmed black bodies being gunned down by police that fuel #BLM are recent examples of the moral compass of much of America.

As a result of this moral preference for victims, even the powerful often claim to be victims in order to win popular support. Presidents of the United States, for instance, who hold, perhaps, the most powerful political office in the world are not above claiming to be a victim of media fabrications, misrepresentations, and bias. No matter how rich and powerful you become, to be morally right often means assuming the role of the victim.

This unspoken assumption in American culture is imagined to be true for every place and time. Surprisingly, however, that is not the case. In other, admittedly, foreign cultures, like the culture described by classical Greek drama, strength was a moral virtue and weakness a vice. From the Trojan War to Odysseus the "sacker of cities," to Achilles, who was dipped in the river Styx by his heels and who met his demise through his only weakness, strength was heroized in ancient Greek culture. In other words, not every culture ascribes the moral high ground to the victims. In some cultures, strength more closely aligns to the image of god(s), while weakness demonstrates a lack of divine favor and personal virtue.

The story of David and Goliath is often read as though David were the underdog. Again, imagining David as a helpless, small boy fighting a giant makes sense in a culture like ours, which labels aggression from the powerful as "bullying." For David to be in the right, we assume, he must be the underdog defeating the bully.

David, however, was no underdog.[41] In fact, just the opposite is true. In biblical times, military personnel were divided into three categories. Infantry were the foot soldiers (2 Samuel 10:6), cavalry rode horseback (Job 39), and archers used bows and arrows as well as slingshots (2 Samuel 7:24).

Military strategy in antiquity was often like a game of rock-paper-scissors. Infantry with close range tactics and heavy spears and armor could overwhelm cavalry; cavalry could often outmaneuver archers; and the archers could defeat infantry from long distances.

David was a skilled archer, while Goliath was an infantry man. In an attempt to avoid a prolonged and bloody battle, they decided to pit the best warrior from each side against one another. For the single match fight, the Philistines, imagining hand to hand combat, chose their largest and strongest infantry man.

When David saw Goliath, outfitted as he was in infantry armor that provided cover from head to

---

[41] For a fuller treatment of Goliath as the underdog, see Malcolm Gladwell's *David and Goliath: Underdogs, Misfits, and the Art of Battling Giants*, Little, Brown, 2013.

toe, he recommended to King Saul: "Your servant will go to fight with this Philistine."[42]

This origin story of King David was not meant to establish him as a weaker underdog. This story was meant to establish David as a powerful military strategist. The fully armored infantry man, Goliath, did his best to approach David, but David kept his distance.

Finally, taking a small stone from his pouch, and placing it in the leather of his sling, David aimed for the small opening in Goliath's helmet that allowed him to see. With a small stone projectile slung until it approached the speed of a bullet, David delivered the fatal blow to the giant's temple. Goliath never stood a chance.

By the next chapter we read, "Saul has killed his thousands, and David his ten thousands."[43] The David and Goliath story marked the beginning of David's military career, after which King Saul "made him a commander of a thousand . . . [and] David had success in all his undertakings."[44] David was neither a victim nor an underdog. He was a man who had extraordinary military capabilities.

---

[42] 1 Samuel 17:32.

[43] 1 Samuel 18:7.

[44] 1 Samuel 18:13ff.

When David was finally anointed King over Israel,[45] he decided to build a Temple to God. Amazingly, however, God said no! From 1 Kings 5, we know that David's plan "to gather together the aliens who were residing in the land of Israel" was to conscript them into forced labor. In other words, David planned to build a temple to the God who freed the slaves by using slave labor.

God's answer was final. "The word of the Lord came [saying,] "you have shed much blood and have waged great wars; you shall not build a house to my name, because you have shed so much blood in my sight on earth.""[46]

In a strange twist, violence and slavery were the foundations upon which the Temple was built. David's son, Solomon, eventually built the Temple, using forced slave labor to do the job.[47] According to the book of Kings, thirty thousand slaves were conscripted to build a temple to the God who freed the slaves. The irony is unmistakable.

---

[45] 2 Samuel 5:3.

[46] 1 Chronicles 22:8ff.

[47] 1 Kings 5:13.

Two Camps: Prophets Against Priests

The irony certainly did not get past the prophet Jeremiah. Jeremiah was descended from a priestly line, himself. However, *that* entire line of priests, save one, was murdered by Israel's royal family.[48] Fearful that the priests would go against the throne, King Saul commanded all of the holy men to be slain. The one priest who managed to escape the deadly plot was the ancestor of Jeremiah. No doubt the prophet heard many tales growing up about the corruption of the throne.

David eventually appointed a new priestly line, the line of Zadok.[49] Yet, the die was cast. The tension between temple religion and the prophets came to a breaking point. Jeremiah warned that the new royal priesthood was acting the way civil religion always acts. It did what patriot pastors do best. It blurred the line between an earthly nation and the kingdom of God.

Jeremiah left a record: "Then I spoke to the priests [in the line of Zadok] and to all the people, saying, "Thus says the Lord: Do not listen to the words of your prophets who are prophesying to you... for they are prophesying a lie to you."[50] The divergent

---

[48] 1 Samuel 22:17–20.

[49] 1 Chronicles 24.

[50] Jeremiah 27:16ff.

voices of the Hebrew Bible take shape in the tension between the Davidic priests and the prophets who spoke out against them.

The lie of which Jeremiah spoke was the priestly claim that David's kingdom would live forever, regardless of the nation's moral character.[51] The priests taught that God was a God of empire, while the prophets taught that God was a liberating God. In other words, Jeremiah accused the monarchy of forgetting the God of the Exodus, the God who takes sides with the poor.

Like Jeremiah, the other prophets of the Old Testament are almost always at odds with temple religion and the outcomes of Empire. As Amos 5 so eloquently remembers God saying, "I hate, I despise your festivals, and I take no delight in your solemn assemblies. Even though you offer me your burnt offerings and grain offerings, I will not accept them . . . Take away from me the noise of your songs; I will not listen to the melody of your harps." *I cannot stress enough how much the prophets were at odds with the priests.*

Why the divine critique of temple worship? "Because you trample on the poor and take from them their levies of grain." Israel allowed the poor to languish, while the rich got richer. They forgot that true worship demands that "justice roll down

---

[51] 2 Samuel 7:16.

like waters."[52] This very same tension between temple priests and God's love for the poor will become apparent in the teachings of Jesus, who seemed constantly at odds with the Pharisees, Sadducees, and other representatives of the temple.

---

[52] Amos 5:24.

Chapter 4: JUBILEE JUSTICE IN JONAH AND THE WHALE

Enemy Love in Jonah

Jonah is one of the places in the Hebrew Bible that expresses God's heart for enemy love. The story reveals a God whose love for enemies feels like a betrayal of his chosen people. Recall that the divine choice to forgive the Assyrians for all the violence they committed upon Israel "was very displeasing to Jonah, and he became angry."[53] "That is why I fled to Tarshish at the beginning; for I knew that you are a gracious God and merciful, slow to anger, and abounding in steadfast love."[54] It is interesting that this beloved verse is actually about Jonah not being able to stomach the grace of God.

An important detail concerning the sacred fish tale is that Jonah was a prophet of the Northern Kingdom. Much like the Civil War in America,

---

[53] Jonah 4:1.

[54] Jonah 4:2.

Israel had its own internal conflict when Solomon's son became King. Israel was in the North, and Judah (think Jew-dah) was in the South. When Assyria finally conquered the Northern Kingdom of Israel, the people there accommodated their religion to Assyrian gods. They intermarried and, essentially, lost their Jewish identity.

The remaining Jews in Judah resented the Northern Kingdom's unfaithfulness. In fact, the animosity between the northern residents of Israel and the southern Jewish residents of Judah was so long-lived that it was still alive and well roughly five hundred years after the gospels were written.

The story of *The Good Samaritan* is meant to be shocking, since every Jew knew that no Samaritan (Samaria being the capital city of the former Israel) could ever be the good guy in a story. Readers of Jonah would have picked up on Jonah's Northern Kingdom, Samaritan identity immediately. No wonder Jonah ran away from God! That's just history repeating itself. That's exactly what Judah expected everyone in the Northern Kingdom to do.

Prophetic Satire

Perhaps the most amazing thing about the story of Jonah, the Northern King prophet who eventually does what God commands when Judah never could, is how unbelievably successful it all is. Assyria, of all places, listened to the Samaritan-like prophet from the North. The foreign king obeyed God.

If you have spent much time reading the Hebrew prophets from the Southern Kingdom of Judah, you know that they were, by and large, failures. Matthew pulls no punches when he remembers what Jesus said about them: "And you say, 'If we had lived in the days of our ancestors, we would not have taken part with them in shedding the blood of the prophets.'"[55] When Jesus pointed out the people's failure to listen to God, the people "were filled with rage," and tried to hurl him off a cliff.[56] "Jerusalem, Jerusalem, the city that kills the prophets and stones those who are sent to it."[57] The takeaway about the Hebrew prophets is that no one heeded their warnings. Yet the story of Jonah is of a pagan king from hated Assyria doing what they never could, following the instructions of Jonah, a prophet from the God-forsaken North.

---

[55] Matthew 23:30.

[56] Luke 4:28.

[57] Matthew 23:37.

This great irony in Jonah is why it fits well into the literary genre of satire. One definition of satire is "the use of humor, irony, exaggeration, or ridicule to expose and criticize people's stupidity or vices, particularly in the context of contemporary politics and other topical issues." Jonah is written as a satirical piece intended to expose the failure of Judah to listen to the prophets. In other words, they failed to recognize that God's concern was not one of state, but of liberation.

The message that Jonah delivered to the King of Assyria was simple: "All shall turn from their evil ways and from the violence that is in their hands."58 Over and over again, whether it be against the violence committed by Pharaoh or Assyria's king or even the chosen people, the prophetic word is the same: "Stop it!"

---

58 Jonah 3:8.

Chapter 5:
REMEMBER JUBILEE AS SABBATH

The Heart of the Gospel

When Jesus quoted the Hebrew Bible, he quoted those prophets discussed above: Jeremiah (Matthew 21:13, Mark 11:17, Luke 19:45), Jonah (Matthew 12:38-41, Mark 8:34-38, Luke 11:29–32), Moses (Mark 12:26, Luke 20:37, John 6:32), as well as others that proclaim God's care for the vulnerable. This is so important for understanding this book. The prophets highlighted in these pages are the same voices highlighted by Jesus Christ. *Far from random voices selected to make a point, these are the voices in the Hebrew Bible that Jesus held up as exemplars of God's heart.* These are the ones who, as Isaiah put it, proclaimed "the year of the Lord's favor" for the most vulnerable.

For Jesus, "all the law and the prophets hang on these two commands," to love God (Deuteronomy 11:1) and to love your neighbor (Leviticus 19:18), both laws traditionally ascribed to Moses. This love, however, was not just the feel-good, easy kind of love. Godly love actually costs something, and the bill came due every Jubilee year.

In much the same way that American culture upholds the ideal of democracy, the Hebrews upheld the ideal of Jubilee. Having only one purpose, the Jubilee year was the power of God to liberate those who, whether through bad luck, poor decisions, sheer laziness, or whatever else, had found themselves down on their luck, indebted, or enslaved.

In biblical times, there were no government welfare programs. As a result, individuals and families would often sell themselves into slavery just to have food to eat. Much like the practice of indentured servitude common in early American history, those who felt they were without other options would voluntarily become slaves. We see this underlying assumption in the story of Jacob, for instance, who sold himself into servitude for seven years in order to marry Rachel. When Laban covered Leah's face and tricked Jacob into marrying her instead, Jacob worked another seven years to earn the right to marry Rachel.[59]

---

[59] Genesis 29:25ff. To explore how women were often abused in the biblical patriarchy, see Phyllis Trible's *Text of Terror* (Minneapolis, MN: Fortress Press, 1984).

It is easy to imagine how harsh realities would leave families with few choices. Famine was a constant threat in biblical times. Crop failures were often a matter of life and death. Borrowing money, combined with a few years of bad weather (a.k.a. failed crops) could mean an inability to repay debts. Land used as collateral would go to the lender, and families would be obligated to repay.

We find this very story in one of Jesus' so-called *parables* (though Jesus never called it that). In Matthew 18 a man owed the equivalent of ten million dollars. If it is a parable, it's not far from reality. Landowners frequently found themselves in such positions if they, having so few options, borrowed money at exorbitant interest rates. Soon, the amount owed would climb to outrageous levels. So, Jesus tells of a lender-king who demanded payment, while the borrower begged for mercy. "And out of mercy for him, the [lender-king] . . . forgave him the debt."[60] This so-called parable is the story of a lender who practiced Jubilee. He forgave the debt that was owed him.

Of course, rich people didn't get rich by being imprudent. It didn't take them long to do the math. If you lend in year six, then chances are high that you will lose it all in the Jubilee. As the "year of the Lord's favor" drew closer and closer, prudent

---

[60] Matthew 18:27.

lenders saw no profit in lending. As a result, credit froze. In response to this, the law commanded lenders, "Be careful that you do not entertain a mean thought, thinking, 'The seventh year of remission is near,' and therefore view your needy neighbor with hostility and give nothing."[61]

In this same chapter of Deuteronomy are the almost identical words that Jesus spoke: "You will always have the poor among you" (John 12:8). In Deuteronomy, though, the meaning is easier to see. "Since there will never cease to be some in need among the earth, I therefore command you, 'Open your hand to the poor and needy neighbor in your land . . . Provide liberally out of your flock, your threshing floor, and your wine press.'"[62] The reference to the poor always being among us is meant to highlight the ever-present opportunity to practice the costly love of Jubilee.

In Jeremiah we see a time when Jubilee was *almost* practiced (Jeremiah 43:15ff). "You yourselves recently repented and did what was right in my sight by proclaiming liberty to one another . . . but then you turned around and profaned my name when you took back your male and female slaves, who you had set free."

---

[61] Deuteronomy 15:9.

[62] Deuteronomy 15:11ff.

In much the same way that the ideal of democracy has never been fully realized in America,[63] Jubilee is the ideal that was never fully realized in scripture.

Reading the gospels with Jubilee in mind explains so much. When the Law of Jubilee in Leviticus required that fields be left fallow every seventh year, the question was asked, "What shall we eat in the seventh year, if we may not sow or gather in our crop?"[64] In another unmistakable connection to a Jesus with Jubilee on his heart, he says, "Do not worry, saying 'what shall we eat.'"[65] The Jubilee law assures that God "will order [God's] blessing for you in the sixth year, so that it will yield a crop for three years. When you sow in the eighth year, you will be eating from the old crop," Leviticus explained. Similarly, Jesus answered, "Do not worry... Is not life more than food... Look at the

---

[63] To say that democracy has never been fully realized in America does not merely point to the ways that specific races and genders have been excluded in the past. It isn't even intended to stress the fact that if "Didn't Vote" ran for president, s/he would have won every election in the past hundred years. The promise buried deep in the word "Democracy" (meaning literally "rule by the people") is that every person's voice matters. Instead, even among the votes that are counted, America's Constitutional Republic practices representative democracy rather than pure democracy, such that individual citizens do not vote on specific legislation. Pure democracy, for various reasons, has never been fully realized.

[64] Leviticus 25:20.

[65] Matthew 6:25.

---

birds of the air; they neither sow nor reap nor gather in barns, and yet your heavenly Father feeds them."[66] Jubilee was not just a time for canceling debts and freeing the enslaved, it was also a time to experience complete reliance on God's providence and care.

Simplifying to the extreme: **the gospel is that God has determined to end exploitation, subjugation, and domination in all of its death-dealing forms.** Mark calls this gospel "The Kingdom of God" come upon us.[67] Matthew refers to it as "The Kingdom of Heaven."[68] Their point, however, is the same. The rule of God is at hand.[69] And that rule will put a final end to every despot. It will free every slave. It will release every captive. It will mean the divine liberation promised in Isaiah 61 and inaugurated in Luke 4. In the Hebrew Bible, this gospel goes by the name "Jubilee."

---

[66] Matthew 6:25ff.

[67] Mark 1:14–15.

[68] Matthew 3:2.

[69] Mark 1:15 and Matthew 3:2.

Priestly Undoing of Sabbath

Luke's gospel remembers the Lord's prayer with Jubilee clarity. Teaching his disciples how to pray, Jesus uses unmistakable Jubilary language: "Give us this day our daily bread, and forgive us our debts, for we forgive everyone indebted to us."[70] Or in Luke's "Sermon on the Plain." "If you lend to those to whom you expect repayment, what credit is that to you? Even sinners lend to sinners expecting to be repaid fully. But lend to them without expecting to get anything back."[71]

Even in those places where we might imagine Jesus is arguing against stringent enforcement of Sabbath laws, the Jubilee provides another possibility. When Jesus was around five years old, a Jewish rabbi by the name of Hillel added something called the *prosbul* to Jewish law. The *prosbul* was a contract that a borrower would sign saying that they would pay back any loan, thereby agreeing to forgo any Jubilee remission of the debt.[72] Signed by a witness and a judge, the *Mishna* preserves the language of the *prosbul.* "I (so and so) transfer to you (so and so), the judges (in such and such a place), my right to a debt, so that you may recover

---

[70] Luke 11:3, 4.

[71] Luke 6:34ff.

[72] See page 29 of Andre Trocme's *Jesus and the Nonviolent Revolution,* Plough Publishing House, 2003.

---

any amount which (so and so) owes me, at whatever time I will so desire."[73] The purpose of the *prosbul* was to allow debt collection even during the year of Jubilee.

When Jesus denounced the scribes and Pharisees, he insisted that "They tie up heavy burdens, hard to bear, and lay them on the shoulders of others; but they themselves are unwilling to lift a finger to remove them."[74] Knowing about the *prosbul*, it is not hard to imagine the type of burdens that were laid upon the shoulders of others. While the Pharisees were insisting that no grain be plucked on the Sabbath,[75] Jesus was proclaiming an even more stringent Sabbath than the Pharisees prescribed. "For you tithe mint, dill, and cumin, and have neglected the weightier matters of the law: justice, mercy, and faith."[76] It wasn't Jesus who was lax on the Sabbath.[77] It was those who circumvented Jubilee, and thereby kept the Sabbath from doing its liberating work.

---

[73] See page 30 of Andre Trocme's *Jesus and the Nonviolent Revolution*, Plough Publishing House, 2003.

[74] Matthew 23:4.

[75] Matthew 12:1–8.

[76] Matthew 23:23.

[77] Matthew 12:3.

The gospel that Jesus proclaimed was not new. "The Lord spoke to Moses *on Mount Sinai*, saying: Speak to the people of Israel and say to them: When you enter the land that I am giving you, the land shall observe a sabbath for the Lord. Every six years you shall . . . Every fiftieth year you shall . . .."[78] Sunday School might have us believe that the only instruction Moses received on that mountain top were ten commandments. Leviticus, however, remembers that God gave Moses much more than law. Moses brought down good news. In fact, the message that Moses heard was very much like the gospel proclaimed by Jesus: relief for the poor, release for the captive, and freedom for the oppressed (Luke 4:18–19). In a word, Jubilee.

---

[78] Leviticus 25:1ff.

PART TWO: JUBILEE AFTER THE HEBREW BIBLE

Chapter 6:
RESURRECTION
AND JUBILEE

The End of Violence

There is a fascinating story that recounts Jesus arguing with Sadducees over the resurrection. The Sadducees did not believe in the existence of the resurrection partly because they only considered the first five books of the Old Testament authoritative. Since those books say nothing about resurrection, the Sadducees rejected it outright.[79] So, hoping to embarrass Jesus publicly, they decided to ask him a question that would expose how absolutely ridiculous resurrection belief really is:

"Whose wife shall she be?"[80]

---

[79] In the earliest writings of the Bible, everyone goes to the same place after they die. That place in Hebrew is called *Sheol* and is most commonly interpreted as "the grave." Whether it was the much-hated King of Babylon (Isaiah 14:9) or the beloved patriarch, Jacob (Genesis 37:35), *Sheol* was the final resting place for all. "Whatever your hand finds to do, do with all your might; for there is no work or thought or knowledge or wisdom in *Sheol*, to which you are going" (Ecclesiastes 9:10).

[80] Matthew 22:28.

The question being asked regarded something called Levirate marriage, which were laws that required a woman to marry her brother-in-law should her husband die.

The Sadducees set their trap. They described a woman who experienced an inordinate amount of grief. After losing her first husband, her second husband soon died, then her third, and so on, until the final brother-number-seven married her.

"Whose wife will she be in heaven?" In this story, intended to trap Jesus by exposing what they considered the silliness of resurrection, the Sadducees neglected to pay attention to the brutal life the woman had experienced. According to a harsh, patriarchal system that treated women as property, this hypothetical "wife" was passed from one "owner" to another.

Avoiding the trap and exposing the heartlessness of the question, Jesus responded to the cruelty of human ownership. Whose wife will she be? "You know neither the scriptures nor the power of God," Jesus answered. "For in the resurrection [women] neither marry nor are given in marriage."[81] *Whatever the resurrection is, it resembles the Jubilee proclamation* that no human will be owned by another. Resurrection is a state in which the

[81] Matthew 22:29–30.

captives are released and the oppressed are truly set free, because God is a liberating God.

Chapter 7: PAUL'S LIBERATION FROM TOXIC RELIGION

Paul is not ashamed to name himself among the Apostles (2 Corinthians 11:5), but the title *Reformer* may be equally appropriate. Though the label *Reformer* in Western history is typically reserved for those sixteenth-century-and-on personalities like Luther, Calvin, and Zwingli, examining his Reformer's heart actually helps us to understand Paul, too.

The Reformer Paul lived in an agrarian (meaning non-capitalist, and often food-insecure) society. The technological innovations that capitalism has, in large part, made possible (like tractors that can do the work of thirty men) assists individuals a great deal in farming land all on their own. Capitalism (among other forces) has created such great wealth in America that it is natural for us to teach our children to grow up and leave the nest. Parents expect their children to become economically independent. This independence training, however, was not possible in Paul's time. Biblical culture was characterized by dependence training, not independence training.

In *The Death of Adam*, Marilynne Robinson coined the phrase "the creation of childhood." For nearly all of human history, she wrote, by the tender age of five or six children were expected to labor on the farm. Not until the modern period and its labor laws did childhood take on the image of learning and leisure.

When Jesus called the (adult) disciples (Matthew 4:33), most worked for the family business. They were in the boat with their fathers, for instance. Even parables expressed the generational families that constituted agrarian life in biblical times. The prodigal son is one such example.[82]

Extended families lived and worked together as an economic unit, because that is how they survived the vicissitudes of life in antiquity. The idea of becoming economically independent from your family in agrarian cultures would have been out of place and time, generally speaking.

Life required a support structure. To have no family and no community, therefore, was death-dealing. And it was in this setting that Paul's understanding of the gospel took shape. It is important to recognize that nowhere in all of Paul's letters did he ever once directly mention Jubilee. Nonetheless, as the following will demonstrate, Paul was every bit a Jubilee preacher!

---

[82] Luke 15:11–32.

Paul Going the Way of Purgatory

According to one author, Paul's emphasis on the law is fast becoming irrelevant. The exact same thing happened with much of Luther's Reformation subject matter. His insistence that paying indulgences to get people an early parole out of Purgatory has lost any relevance to modern day Protestants. Ask any Baptist, Methodist, Presbyterian, or Lutheran today what their opinions are on Purgatory, and you'll likely get a blank stare. For Luther, though, it was of such religious significance that it created irreparable fractures in a millennia-plus old Catholic, Holy Roman Empire religion. Today, Paul's obsessive concern over legal justification may quickly be going the way of Purgatory.

He wrote an inordinate amount on the topic of justification by faith and went on and on giving legal descriptions about how one gains citizenship in God's kingdom. Justice (a legal term) must be made. The debt (also a legal term) must be paid if a righteous God is to be satisfied. Elements of substitutionary atonement and penal substitution are found in Paul's work; again, both grounded in legal language. But is this legalistic language of Paul's becoming less and less meaningful?

Professor and Pastor, Gerhard O. Forde was, perhaps, correct when he insisted that we contemporary readers have a hard time finding Paul's legal concerns relevant. They mattered to Paul's audience, Forde noted, because Paul lived in a culture that held very clear, unquestioned moral values. But such unquestioned moral values, Forde argued, no longer exist.

Forde was pointing to the work that psychologists and sociologists have done to absolve individuals of their guilt in the modern age. Sigmund Freud did a lot to relocate responsibility for bad behavior. In our culture, "The devil made me do it" is slowly but surely being replaced with, "My behavior is a product of my upbringing." Examples abound.

For Your Own Good is a book written by Alice Walker that suggests the roots of violence begin with parental spanking. Parents are largely to blame for the easy relationship moderns have with violence, she says. Walter Wink noted how generations have grown up watching cartoons that teach the myth of redemptive violence. Whether it's the Coyote getting the karmic anvil on the head for all his dastardly plotting, or every Marvel superhero who saves the day by beating and sometimes killing "bad guys," we tend to heroize and glorify violence.[83] bell hooks argued that men are trained

---

[83] See Walter Wink's *The Powers That Be*, Double Day, New York, London, 1998 page 43.

from a very early age to stunt their emotions.[84] "Real men don't cry" is something nearly every young man has heard. Men are enculturated into muting emotions that society deems effeminate. When men engage in emotionally immature behavior, culture is largely to blame since it disallows the full spectrum of male emotional responses, hooks argued. In the eighteenth century, Saint Simon noted the correlation between certain kinds of crime and poverty. Thievery, he noted, is partly a product of social and economic policies that leave people destitute.

The point of all this is to say that blame has increasingly been relocated away from the perpetrators of bad behavior and placed, instead, on caregiving moms and dads, culture, public policy, or some other culprit. It is with great wisdom that psychologists and social scientists are better understanding the complexities of human behavior. But what does this mean for the religious principle of guilt?

What happens to the concept of "sin" when individuals are no longer to blame for their own misdeeds? As Rodgers and Hammerstein famously wrote, "We have to be taught, before it's too late, before we are six or seven or eight, to hate all the

---

[84] See Bell Hooks' *The Will to Change: Men, Masculinity, and Love*, Atria Books, New York, London, Toronto, Sydney, 2004.

---

people our relatives hate. We have to be carefully taught."[85] In a society that increasingly complexifies the very idea of individual sin, the language of individual justification is becoming less and less meaningful.

Added to all of this is the continued loss of an unwavering standard of moral values. One church denies women the ability to speak in the service. Another has a female bishop. One congregation has a married, lesbian pastor, while the church across the street condemns same sex relationships.

This, however, is not limited to religious institutions. Secular "moral stories" have come under suspicion as well. At the time of this writing, *Columbus Day* is now *Indigenous People's Day* in Alaska, New Mexico, Hawaii, and Maine. The heroes of America's national origins are simultaneously villains. Again, how does the language of justification make sense in a culture and religion that has no unquestionable moral standard?

None of this changes the fact that Paul's letters seem overwhelmingly interested in the legalistic language of justification. What it does do, however, is shed light on why those parts of Paul's letters seem less relevant in the twenty-first century. This

---

[85] Hammerstein, Oscar, Richard Rodgers, and Joshua Logan. *South Pacific: A Musical Play*. 1949.

is especially true regarding the uninitiated who have to first be taught what it means to be guilty of sin. After all, America's "unaffiliated," uninitiated, "nones" are outgrowing every other religious category. The grand narrative of guilt is under a great deal more suspicion than it has ever been before.

Ironically, the enormity of space that Paul dedicated in his letters to the subject of "justification" is intended to make the point that the legal stuff isn't even necessary. It has been done away with. Sin, guilt, judgment, and condemnation have all been nailed to the cross, so to speak. It has all been dealt with decisively by a liberating God.

Paul and the "*Kindom*"

In what may be the easiest-to-understand of all his legal goings on, Paul used the language of adoption to explain what justification meant.[86] In Romans 8:15, he put it this way: For you have not received "a spirit of slavery," but you have received a "spirit of adoption." Paul's entire point in all his talk about legalism and justification is to say that "all who are led by the Spirit are children of God."[87]

Biblical verses such as these inspired Cuban-American theologian Ada María Isasi-Diaz to use the term *kindom* rather than kingdom when talking about God's reign. To be adopted is to be grafted into a family.

In clear contrast to the typical ways nations use the word kingdom, replete with sanctioned violence in the name of keeping the "peace" (I place this word in quotation marks to acknowledge the irony of a militarily-enforced "peace"), the kingdom language of western colonial empires has always meant socio-economic stratification and violence.

This, however, is not the "*kindom* of God" that Paul meant. Where Jesus is "Christ" or ruler, there is no distinction between male and female, Greek or Jew,

---

[86] Galatians 4:5.

[87] Romans 8:14.

slave, or master.[88] Social distinctions around gender (patriarchy), ethnicity (racism), and economic standing (poverty) are all eliminated under God's *kindom* rule.

In Leviticus 25, we learn that Jubilee was the name of the divine command to set free the oppressed and subjugated, and then to reorder society in a way that restores the equity that God intended for all of God's people. It is easy to see, then, that although the word Jubilee is absent, the practice of Jubilee in Paul's letters is unmistakable.

---

[88] Galatians 3:28.

Paul's Reformation

As the son of a Pharisee[89] and zealous advocate of Pharisaic Judaism,[90] Paul's understanding of the law was grounded in the religious tradition of his family.[91] One is not a pastor for very long without meeting very lovely people who have had very bad experiences with family religion. Oftentimes, harsh and unloving parents have used the Bible to justify cruelty and outright abuse inflicted upon their children.

Sometimes it is as simple as making children feel judged and unloved. Other times, the Bible becomes a bludgeon in the hands of parents who condemn their children for things like sexuality[92] or divorce.

Paul eventually came to see the religion of his father as deeply oppressive. There are yet no historical-psychoanalytical studies exposing the Apostle Paul's daddy issues, so rigorous scholarship provides few insights. *The Hero's*

---

[89] Acts 23:6.

[90] Philippians 3:5–6.

[91] Philippians 3:5. Paul states plainly that his relationship to the Law is firmly established in his identity as a Pharisaic Jew.

[92] The Jubilee nature of sexuality in Paul's letters is explored below. See *Paul, Sex, and Liberation*.

Journey, however, shines a great light on the narrative arc of Paul's life.

Joseph Campbell's insights into the literary structure of the hero's journey provides an inviting lens through which to imagine Paul more clearly.[93] His supernatural conversion experience[94] led him out into adventure, to the life-threatening trials of floggings,[95] shipwrecks,[96] and prison.[97] Paul's epic journey was fraught with danger and temptation. He crossed a threshold, such that he was no longer in the safety, security, and comfort his father's world provided him.

The religious tradition he inherited from his father wasn't only an obstacle to living faithfully,[98] though it certainly was that. Paul came to see that it

---

[93] See Joseph Campbell's *The Hero's Journey*, New World Library, Novato, California, 1990

[94] Acts 9. Interestingly, in Paul's own body of work, he never mentions this conversion experience.

[95] 2 Corinthians 11:25.

[96] Acts 27:39ff. See also 2 Corinthians 11:25.

[97] Acts 16:16ff.

[98] Romans 14:13ff. Paul insists that "the kingdom of God is not food and drink," referring to dietary laws, "but righteous and peace and joy in the Holy Spirit." Paul goes on to say that whether you eat meat sacrificed to idles is not important. The important thing is, that whether you do or not, you do it to build up the kingdom.

was also death-dealing. As he wrote in one of his letters to the Church in Corinth, the law kills![99]

---

[99] 2 Corinthians 3:6.

The Law that Kills

The idea that the letter of the law kills is not, for Paul, merely a spiritual platitude. The stories of Paul's years as "persecutor of the church"[100] recount in his own voice that he "violently" persecuted the church and tried to "destroy it." Paul "was ravaging the church by entering house after house; dragging off both men and women [and] committing them to prison."[101]

To be clear, a prison sentence was often a death sentence. Unlike modern, commercial, for-profit prisons, in which prisoners are often given nutritious meals, free medical attention, and cable television, prisons in antiquity were under no obligation to provide food and water to the imprisoned; and often, they did not. When Jesus recounts in Matthew 25 that caring for the imprisoned was the same thing as caring for him, he knew that without regularly visiting caretakers bringing life-giving sustenance, a prison sentence was often a death sentence.

But the law that kills did not always take the prison route. Another story of Paul's pre-conversion violence involved the murder of Saint Stephen, often referred to as the first martyr of Christianity.

---

[100] Galatians 1:13.

[101] Acts 8:3.

The stoning of Stephen in Acts 7 recounts Paul in a trusting relationship with the execution squad. Paul was put in charge of watching over their personal property. In today's legal vernacular, we might call him an accomplice, like the one keeping the car running while the men with guns go into the bank. At the very least, as the ESV version puts it, "[Paul] approved of his execution."[102] Overall, it is fair to say that Paul witnessed, approved, and participated in the literal death-dealing religion of his father.

Given that family and community were required for staying alive in antiquity, Rabbi Berkun's commentary on Leviticus 12:1–13:59 is also instructive. The story of the Good Samaritan is a reminder that Jewish law prohibited contact with a dead body. As the Psalmist notes, *God is the source of life. The God of Israel embodies life, and only the living can praise God.*[103] "Therefore, encounters with death *or symbolic reminders of death* momentarily remove us from the life affirming rituals of God's abode in the Temple." Taken to the extreme, such legal realities left those most in need of healing on the margins. Leprosy, for instance, was not fatal. It did, however, leave the body with a corpse-like appearance.[104]

---

[102] Acts 8:1. According to the NRSV, "Saul approved of their killing him."

[103] Psalm 115:16–17.

[104] Leviticus 13.

The reason the Priest and the Levite in Luke 10:25 left the man in the ditch to languish was that contact with death left one impure.[105] Rather than risk exclusion from religious ritual, the mediators of God's law thought it best to leave a person for dead.

The language in Matthew 8 of Jesus declaring the leper clean, then, was more than just a story of supernatural healing. The disease wasn't fatal, but being declared unclean most certainly could be! The healing of a leper meant the excluded could finally be restored to his support system, his family, and his community. Or again, in Matthew 15, a crowd of four thousand gathered, including "the lame, the maimed, the blind, [and] the mute."[106] Only after specifically naming the infirmed among the crowd does Jesus say, "I have compassion for the crowd for they have been with me for three days and have nothing to eat; and I do not want to send them away hungry, for they might faint on the way." In true ableist form, physical maladies of all sorts could have the consequence of marginalizing those most in need of care. Taken to the extreme, the business of ritual impurity often resulted in brutal conditions for those familiar with desperate

---

[105] Leviticus 19. See also Number 19:11, where coming into contact with a dead body makes one unclean.

[106] Matthew 15:30.

---

need; another death-dealing feature of Paul's childhood faith.

The letter of the law, then, was not merely a means of spiritual death. It was an implement of religious terror. Rather than furthering a Jewish gospel of Jubilee, *the religion of Paul's father was marked by brutality. In other words, it embodied the very death-dealing conditions that Jubilee was designed to remedy. Namely, the conditions that exploit, neglect, and dehumanize those who are the most vulnerable in society.*

It is of the utmost importance to recognize that Paul's critique was not of the Jewish faith. His critique was aimed at Pharisee-*ism*. It was against the kind of religious extremism that leaves a wake of suffering in its path. Much like Luther and other Reformers, Paul took issue with how the Jewish Bible was being interpreted. In fact, the separation between Jewish and Christian had not yet fully taken place when Paul wrote most of his letters.

In her book titled *Paul was not a Christian*, Jewish scholar Pamela Eisenbaum made a compelling argument that Paul (like Luther) never intended to establish a new faith. He was, rather, a devout Jew, working to clarify the life-giving, covenantal faith proclaimed in Hebrew scripture. The problem was not the Jewish religion. The problem was its most lethal, extremist interpretations.

Supper and Jubilee

Paul's concern was that the Jewish religion had become complicit in the perpetuation of those conditions that compelled voluntary slavery as a defense against starvation. It had become complicit in marginalizing the most vulnerable in society. It had become complicit in perpetuating brutality and violence.

As a result, Paul began preaching the Jubilee gospel that Moses had brought down from Mt. Sinai and that the prophets had proclaimed over and over. Again, much like Luther, Paul did not invent anything new. He simply read the good news as it was found in his own religion's holy scriptures. Namely, that God's word and work was about the literal, historical reorganization of the social order toward justice and equity.

Paul's insistence that life with God meant a reorganization of society around justice and equity was not merely spiritual. Much like the community in Acts 2, Paul understood the church to be a gathering that tends to the physical, embodied needs of *all* of God's people.

In what must be one of the most concerning of all the New Testament stories to die hard capitalists, Acts 2 recounts a group of new believers that did something radical. They exchanged an economy of private ownership for a communal one. This cannot be properly understood, however, without emphasizing that the story follows directly after the event of Pentecost, which is the biblical account of God's Spirit coming down from heaven and creating the Church.

The same Luke who remembered the gospel as "the year of the Lord's favor" (in Luke 4) also remembered how the year of the Lord's favor looked for the very first-ever "church." I cannot overstate just how powerful that fact is. The very first thing that the author of Luke-Acts wants readers to know about how receiving the Holy Spirit shapes the life of the Church is that it "inspires" a radically reorganized social and economic order.

"[T]hat day, about three thousand persons were added. They devoted themselves to the apostles' teaching and fellowship . . . all who believed were together and had all things in common; they would sell their possessions and goods and distribute the proceeds to all, as any had need."[107]

There has been a great deal of interest and effort in demonstrating why this text does not mean that *we* should live this way. Such perspectives, though, only increase suspicion that so much of what passes for theology is nothing more than our excuse before God. The Church may have far too much in common with the Rich Young Fool, who was

---

[107] Acts 2:41ff.

unable to think differently about his relationship to material wealth.[108] Ultimately, the importance of the story is not found in the question of capitalism versus socialism.[109] It is found in the living gospel that, "there was not a needy person among them."[110]

Acts 2 is not the only place in scripture we see Church reorganize economic and social lives in the name of the gospel. The Love Feast in 1 Corinthians provides insight into Paul's understanding of God's Jubilee heart.[111]

The earliest account of the Eucharist (also called Communion) is found in Paul's letters. Amazingly, there is no biblical distinction between the Communion marked by the words of institution and the sharing of a full-fledged, potluck style supper-meal together. The same, of course, was true in the gospels, where "This is my body" and "This is my blood" (referred to as "the words of institution") are words spoken at the Passover feast.[112] In the Bible, Communion or Eucharist is not a ritual of empty

---

[108] Luke 12:13–21.

[109] Importantly, these economic philosophies did not exist in biblical times.

[110] Acts 4:34.

[111] Corinthians 11:17ff.

[112] Luke 22:14ff.

calories, of cardboard tasting wafers stamped with a cross, washed down with a tablespoon of grape juice. In the early Church, Communion was an entire supper-meal.

Paul's literal-physical (not metaphorical-spiritual) understanding of Eucharist addressed the very real issues of hunger and poverty (again, as mentioned above, the conditions that fuel the exploitative institution of slavery). Paul was frustrated[113] because he had received a report that the poorest in the community were being left out of the Communion meals.

His response was to demand that eating without considering those who are hungry was a sin. And when you do it, he insisted, you desecrate the sacrament of Eucharist. In other words (and I know this might be shocking), biblically speaking, Communion is not the middle-class altar ritual of bended knee and beautiful cathedral serving up good religious feelings. Rather, Communion is the practice of being close to God by eating a calorie-rich meal with poor, hungry people. There is little distinction between what Jesus said in Matthew 25 and what Paul said in 1 Corinthians 17. The actual bodily presence of Jesus is located in the company of people who need a meal.

---

[113] 1 Corinthians 11:17ff.

Sunday morning's overly spiritualized Communion practices are of zero use for food-insecure people. To their credit, however, some churches understand this, and so consider the worship liturgy to be a rehearsal for what happens when they leave the sanctuary. The ritual of sharing the peace in worship is a rehearsal for being peacemakers when they leave behind the pews and paraments. The ritual of Confession is practice for when they leave the church building to be the peacemakers of the world. And the ritual of Communion is a rehearsal for what comes next; namely, ministries that literally feed, clothe, and care for the bodily needs of those who happen to be in a place of vulnerability in this season of their lives.

So, Paul said, if you're coming to Communion supper just to eat, drink, and get your fill, then "stay home!"[114] Again, Communion is about alleviating the historical, social, and economic conditions that make selling oneself into slavery just to have food to eat seem like a good idea. Biblical Communion was intended to be a remedy for the suffering of actually food-insecure, hungry people. In short, it was exactly what a new-*kindom*-inaugurated looked like when that kingdom was grounded in the good news of Jubilee. Namely, the beginning of the end of those social and economic conditions that leave

---

[114] 1 Corinthians 11:22.

people with little choice but to put themselves in positions where they are likely to be exploited.

Likewise, 2 Corinthians is unmistakably clear. In language remarkably similar to Acts 2, Paul explained what the Church of Christ looks like. Namely, a restructuring of economic reality. "It's a question of a fair balance," Paul wrote, "between your present abundance and their need . . . As it is written 'The one who had much did not have too much, and the one who had little did not have too little.'"[115]

---

[115] 2 Corinthians 8:15.

Paul the Reformer and Kierkegaard

There is an important difference between the Jubilee hope expressed in the Hebrew Bible and the Jubilee hope expressed in Paul's letters. Throughout Hebrew scripture, the primary sources of injustice among society's most vulnerable were the political elites.

The middle class is another consequence of twentieth-century capitalism. Biblical cultures knew almost nothing of a middle class or social mobility. Society was marked by the political elites, whose riches were primarily acquired through various forms of taxation, and the agrarian working class. When the prophets in the Hebrew Bible prophesied against those robbing the poor, they were talking about the political elites.

To clarify, when Amos prophesied against "Israel," the crimes listed were very specific: "Therefore, because you trample on the poor and take from them levies of grain."[116] Again, "because they sell the righteous for silver and the needy for a pair of shoes . . ."[117] The "you" and the "they" who trample on the poor and sell the righteous were the political rulers.

---

[116] Amos 5:11ff.

[117] Amos 2:6ff.

The disaster that Amos was predicting upon Israel as punishment for their sin was, ironically, not putative, but restorative. In other words, disaster was threatened for the benefit of Israel's oppressed. Because rulers "do not know how to do right,"[118] their power would be taken away from them. Afterward, Amos prophesied, God would "repair [Israel's] breaches, and raise up its ruins, and rebuild it as in the days of old."[119] "The time is surely coming, says the Lord, when the one who plows shall overtake the one who reaps... the mountains shall drip sweet wine... I will restore the fortunes of my people... and they shall never be plucked from the land that I have given them."[120] The narrative arc in the writings of the Hebrew prophets involve removing the exploitative and brutal political rulers of Israel *in order to* restore the blessings that God intends for all of God's people.

To Paul, however, it wasn't politics creating the biggest obstacle to Jubilee. Toxic religion was the tool of oppression. As he saw it, those claiming to be bearers of God's law were the greatest threat to what God was actually up to in the world. This distinction is critical to understanding just how

---

[118] Amos 3:10.

[119] Amos 9:11.

[120] Amos 9:13ff.

Jubilee fits into Paul's understanding of the gospel. Paul's diagnosis of human suffering looked different than the slavery and debt named in Leviticus. His sacred scripture knew of injustice caused by political and economic systems, and the solutions to those conditions were religious in nature. The divine command given by God to Moses on the mountain was the remedy for the most vulnerable who were being crushed by debt and poverty.

By Paul's time, however, the catalogue of laws that once worked to right social injustices were now a root cause. Aided by centuries of added tradition, reinterpretation, and commentaries that circumvented the original intent, religion itself became the problem.[121] Paul, however, was not the only individual in history to critique the religion he inherited with a force that permanently changed the trajectory of faith.

Søren Kierkegaard, regarded as the father of existentialism, was a Danish theologian and philosopher who radically altered the trajectory of both philosophy and theology. Born to a Lutheran family, he offered a scathing critique of the Danish church. "We are called a 'Christian' nation," he

---

[121] The Mishna, Gemara, and Talmud contain commentary, hundreds of years in the making, that began as oral tradition. The Pharisees considered oral tradition to have equal weight with the written Torah.

wrote, "but in such a sense that not a single one of us is in the character of the Christianity of the New Testament."[122] Is this not the feeling of every Christian reformer?

Disillusioned by the state of Christianity, and brazen enough to speak his mind, Kierkegaard expressed the dire need that Christ be introduced to the Christian church.[123] Ouch! What might he say about the church today?

---

[122] See *A Kierkegaard Anthology*, Edited by Robert Bretall, © 1946, Princeton University Press, page 437

[123] As Kierkegaard put it, "Christendom has done away with Christianity, without being aware of it. The consequence is that, if anything is to be done, one must try again to introduce Christianity into Christendom." See *A Kierkegaard Anthology*, Edited by Robert Bretall, © 1946, Princeton University Press, page 397.

Chapter 8: PAUL, SEX, AND LIBERATION

God's Resounding "No!"

Though used by many as a proof text to condemn anything other than heterosexual behavior, New Testament comments about sex were actually taking aim at the then socially acceptable practice of pedophilia.[124] In biblical times, it was common in Greco-Roman culture for grown men to use prepubescent boys as sexual slaves. This practice, called *pederasty*, was prevalent in Greco-Roman culture. In Plato's Symposium, for instance, Pausanias explained why men preferred young boys to women.[125]

---

[124] Pauline texts typically associated with issues of sexual "sin" are Romans 1:26–27; 1 Corinthians 6:9–10; and 1 Timothy 1:9–10.

[125] See Plato's Symposium (181 b, c). Pausanias notes that sexual relationships with boys (pederasty) was considered preferable to women. As David M. Halperin noted, when boys started to show signs of puberty, adult males would typically end the relationship. (See *One Hundred Years of Homosexuality and Other Essays on Greek Love*, New York: Routledge, 1990, page 88.

In 1946, for the first time in history, the Greek word *arsenokoitai*,[126] typically translated "pederast," was translated into the English word "homosexual."[127] In fact, that year the Revised Standard Version translation of the Bible combined two Greek words in 1 Timothy 1:10 into the one English word, "homosexual." The two Greek words were, again, *arsenokoitai* ("pederast"), and *malakoi* ("soft" or "effeminate"). The New Revised Standard Version of the Bible did only remotely better in 1989 when it translated 1 Timothy 1:10 as "sodomites and slave traders." At least it recognized the existence of two distinct words.

Far from a condemnation of homosexuality, Timothy was referring to the men who used boys for sex (*arsenokoitai*) and the slave traders who sold them (*malakoi*).[128] The simple truth is that these texts say nothing about the twentieth-century debates concerning same sex relationships.

In 1 Corinthians 6:9, Paul used the same language. His list of vices contained the same pair,

---

[126] 1 Corinthians 6:9 and 1 Timothy 1:10.

[127] In his 1521 German translation, Martin Luther interpreted *arsenokoitai* as *Knabenschander* ("pederasts").

[128] The NIV continues to translate 1 Timothy 10 as "practicing homosexuals and slave traders."

arsenokoitai and *malakoi.*[129] For Paul, too, the common practice of pederasty and the slave traders who profit in pedophilia "will not inherit the Kingdom of God."

In Romans 1, Paul was speaking explicitly about Gentile forms of idolatry. Three times (Romans 1:18, 23, 25) prior to mentioning women who "exchanged natural intercourse for unnatural," Paul made reference to worshipping other gods than the one true God. What other gods did Paul have in mind? Cybele was a fertility goddess, coined "the protector of Rome." Her image was on Roman coinage with the inscription *MATER DEUM*, meaning "mother of the gods." There were multiple temple sites for Cybele worship, including one located where the Vatican now sits. Worship and festivals of the fertility goddess included shrine prostitutes who did every deed Paul mentioned in Romans 1: 26–28, *and more*. As the writer of Ephesians wrote in what is subtitled, *Renouncing Pagan Ways*, "It is shameful to even mention . . ."[130]

The point of such scholarship is less about defending any position concerning contemporary,

---

[129] The Greek-English lexicon of the New Testament indicates the term *malakos* pertains "to being passive in a same-sex relationship, effeminate," University of Chicago Press; 3rd edition, 2001, page 92.

[130] Ephesians 5:12.

same sex, loving, and committed relationships, and more about reclaiming the original meaning of scripture in its own context. In a culture that openly practiced pedophilia, scripture resounds with God's "No!" In a culture that openly practiced dehumanizing, ritual intercourse without love, responsibility, or commitment, scripture resounds with God's "No!"

Here again, the New Testament scriptures concerning sexuality embody a Jubilee vision. They outright reject sexual activities that are exploitative and abusive. Instead, sexuality is meant to be humanizing, other-affirming, self-liberating, socially responsible, and joyous. In other words, the Jubilee proclamation of liberation also concerns sex.

Paul and the Weakness of God

In Paul's letter to the Philippians, he invited his readers to imitate Christ, who "though he was in the form of God… emptied himself… humbled himself and became obedient to the point of death — even death on a cross."[131] To the Church in Galatia he wrote, "May I never boast of anything except the cross of our Lord Jesus Christ."[132] Over and over again Paul presented the cross as the center of gravity around which all his theology revolved. If you want to understand what God is doing in the world, look at the cross, Paul insisted. "For I decided to know nothing among you except Jesus Christ, and him crucified."[133]

When Paul declared that, "There is no one who is righteous, not even one,"[134] he was pointing to how deeply the world is broken. The Bible speaks of this through the narrative of the fall in Genesis 3 and in Paul's letter to the Romans, chapter 5. Many imagine "the fall" as a story of depravity, filled with sex, drugs, and rock 'n' roll. Nothing could be further from the truth.

---

[131] Philippians 2:6–8.

[132] Galatians 6:14.

[133] 1 Corinthians 2:2.

[134] Romans 3:10-12.

The story of the fall is not the story of falling *down*. It is the story of falling *up*! The infamous (and apocryphal) "apple" was just the means. Rather than hoping for a debauch, the hope in Adam and Eve's eating the forbidden fruit was to "be like God."[135] In the story of the fall, the sin that broke creation, the reason that creation is such a mess, is because humans attempted a coup on God's rule. The fall is the story of how humans determined to take God's place!

To be clear, the great sin is not just about doing what's wrong. It's about deciding what's right. As one author put it, "We sin not merely in our vices, but in our virtues."[136] The gospels insist that it was the so-called moral leaders who put Jesus on the cross.[137] They were doing what they thought was right. Claims to "virtue, godliness, wisdom, justice, goodness, and so forth are exactly what put Jesus on the cross."[138] Even our best, most altruistic efforts at creating a better world are fraught with painful, unintended consequences. As the proverb

---

[135] Genesis 3:5.

[136] See Gerhard O. Forde, *Theology is for Proclamation* (Minneapolis, MN: Augsburg Fortress, 1990), 143.

[137] Matthew 26:59.

[138] See Gerhard O. Forde *On Being a Theologian of the Cross* (Grand Rapids, MI: Wm. B. Eerdmans, 1997), 77.

says, "All deeds are right in the sight of the doer, but the Lord weighs the heart."[139]

As such, the cross is not just something one must endure to enter the kingdom. The cross *is* the kingdom come! In other words, God's rule does not begin until our kingdom ends. The kingdom of God means our death. This is what Paul meant when he wrote, "For I have been crucified with Christ, and it is no longer I who live."[140] The cross is the end of our efforts to be our own gods.

---

[139] Proverbs 21:2.

[140] Galatians 2:19, 20.

Paul and the Mountaintop Message

There is a powerful story in Matthew when Jesus was in the Garden of Gethsemane, and Judas-the-betrayer approached him with armed Roman guards, as well as other religious leaders. Peter knew that the guards were there to arrest Jesus, and that it likely meant Jesus' death. So, without thinking, Peter drew his sword.

Now, Peter was no samurai warrior. He was a fisherman. So, he didn't have in mind the precision cut of a practiced swordsman. Most probably, Peter was swinging for the bleachers when he cut off only the ear of the high priest's servant.[141] Kill if I must, Peter reacted, but I will protect what I love.

In response, Jesus said the most remarkable thing to Peter. "Put your sword back into its place… Do you not think that I can appeal to my Father, and he will at once send me more than twelve legions of angels?" The image Jesus painted was unforgettable. A legion is a military term for five- to six-thousand-foot soldiers. Jesus painted a picture of a heavenly army so large that it would have spilled out far beyond the Garden they inhabited. The divine army Jesus described could easily overwhelm Rome. But *that* was not God's way, Jesus said.

---

[141] Matthew 26:51.

Resistance to violence in any form is at the heart of Jubilee. On Gethsemane, it looked like Peter putting away his weapon. For Paul's friend, Philemon, it looked like forgiveness.

Paul's short letter to Philemon is a great example of living out Jubilee in everyday life. "I could command you," Paul insisted. "I am bold enough in Christ to demand you to do your duty, yet I would rather appeal to you on the basis of love."[142] Paul's hope was that Philemon would release Onesimus, "so that you may take him back forever, no longer as a slave…"[143] With this one stroke, Paul made it clear just what the Gospel meant for daily living. "If he has wronged you in any way, or owes you anything, charge that to my account."[144] Paul was appealing for complete and total liberation from slavery *and* remission of debt. Can you get more Jubilee than that?

Paul's claim that "God's weakness is stronger than human strength" was also a reference to the cross.[145] What Jesus inaugurated was so unlike anything we would expect. God rules in weakness,

---

[142] Philemon 1:8.

[143] Philemon 1:16.

[144] Philemon 1:18.

[145] 1 Corinthians 1:25.

not in strength. That means that traveling to the cross where there is weakness, pain, vulnerability, blood, and even death is journeying to the place we find God in this world. Why? Because that is often what the world has to offer those who love unconditionally, who advocate for the weak, stand up for the vulnerable, and take the side of the outcast.

Teachings of Jesus, such as those found in the Sermon on the Mount, are troubling, to say the least. Love your enemy? If someone strikes you, turn the other cheek? If someone steals your coat, give them your shirt as well? Many have tried to interpret these texts so that they tell the story of civil resistance to evil. Yet Jesus clearly says: Do not resist evil.[146]

This nonviolent approach to life ends right where we would expect it to: *at the cross.* And not just for Jesus, but also for those closest to him. All but one disciple died a martyr.[147] The kind of life that Jesus inaugurated was simply not for this world. "From the days of John the Baptizer until now, the Kingdom of Heaven has suffered violence, and the violent take it by force."[148]

---

[146] Matthew 5:39.

[147] Tradition holds that John was the only apostle to die of old age. All others were martyred.

[148] Matthew 11:12.

The problem, of course, is that we want to save our own lives and the lives of those we love. Never mind the impossible claim, "Whoever saves his life will lose it."[149] We know that the kingdom Jesus inaugurated is dangerous. Responding to that danger, the disciple knows that violence in any form is not an option for the people of God. The kingdom of God is a living Jubilee. It's enough to make a disciple confess, "I believe. Help my unbelief."[150]

---

[149] Matthew 16:25.

[150] Mark 9:24

PART THREE: JUBILEE AND THE CHURCH

Chapter 9: JUBILEE AND THE CHURCH

Church and Race

One might think that having (1) myriad prophets in the Hebrew Bible, (2) the New Testament's most prolific writer, the Apostle Paul, and (3) the gospels of Jesus Christ all proclaiming the same message of Jubilee would help make the work of the Church clear. But has it? Churches still struggle with what it means to serve a God who is a liberating God.

One example is the persistent problem of race. "Whiteness" has come under attack in unprecedented ways. That is not a moral claim, but a factual one. Anecdotally, many who are unable to separate their "whiteness" from their essential identity feel themselves under attack. They see critique of whiteness as an attack on them personally, since in their minds they are in their very essence "white!" And they certainly do not imagine themselves as part of a centuries-long conspiracy to keep people of color oppressed.

Perhaps most importantly, many white people do not see "whiteness" for what it is: a relatively recent invention designed to serve economic interests. They haven't been taught that before the Triangular Trade Route, people were identified by ethnicity or religious affiliation, and not by race. Surveys of historical literature reveal that before the enslavement of millions of people from the continent of Africa, white people weren't called "white." They were called Christian, Irish, Norwegian, French, or some other ethnicity or religion.[151] White people only became "white" during the chattel slavery that took root in the 1600s. In other words, the origins of whiteness are tied to blackness, or "negro" in Spanish. By the 1680s, as Winthrop D. Jordan noted, "taking the [English] colonies as a whole, a new term of self-identification appeared — *white*."[152] When white people see their own identity as inseparable from their whiteness instead of seeing "white" as a label invented to further entrench a racist economy, it is a short journey to feeling they (as "white" people) are the victims of reverse racism.

Stephen R.C. Hicks, in his book *Nietzsche and the Nazis*, argues how philosophy served as an accelerant to the violence of the 1930s and 1940s in

---

[151] See Jennifer Harvey's *Dear White Christians: For Those Still Longing for Racial Reconciliation* (Grand Rapids, MI: Wm. B. Eerdmans, 2014), 48ff.

[152] See Winthrow D. Jordan, *The White Man's Burden: Historical Origins of Racism in the United States* (Oxford: Oxford University Press, 1974), 26–27.

Germany, especially Nietzsche's emphasis on the superior morality of the "superman." The ideology of *superman* (or *Übermensch*) became the icon of the superiority of the Aryan race, fueling the racist ideologies that enabled the Shoah.

Philosophy being in the driver's seat is not completely without comparison in today's United States. Much of the rhetoric of America's political turmoil is fueled by a philosophical shift that began in the 1980s. Only instead of bolstering racial prejudice, it deconstructed it. Nietzsche's successors like Jean-Francois Leotard, Michel Foucault, and Jacque Derrida helped provide tools for deconstructing the fiction that "whiteness" is the norm for what is good and fair and just and beautiful. Although that worked to amplify voices in pursuit of racial equity, it also at the same time generated a reactionary culture referred to as "white fragility," which describes the discomfort and defensiveness white people feel when confronted with issues of racial injustice.[153]

Racial economics were part of the narrative of taking Germany back from non-Arians. The Holocaust was an economic program. Education, censorship, and eugenics were tools in Germany's

---

[153] See Robin DiAngelo', White Fragility: Why It's So Hard for White People to Talk About Racism (Boston, MA: Beacon Press, 2018).

economic program.[154] To be sure, to a large extent racism fueled Hitler's rising economy. Many insist that the contemporary political slogan "Make America Great Again" captured a similar momentum. Making America great again was, in many ways for people of color, indistinguishable from making America white again. The slogan is a call to bolster white supremacy and resist the inevitability of a future America in which people of color exorcise political power.

Of course, those who view their identity as inseparable from their whiteness disagree. They aren't racist, they insist! They even have black friends. They just want people of color to behave appropriately. The problem is that they don't recognize how their ideas of "appropriate behavior" are tied to white norms. When they say "behave appropriately," what they want is for people of color to behave like white people behave; to behave as if their experience of America was the same as white people's; to behave as if people of color have the same opportunities as white people; to behave as if hundreds of years of brutal, racist history has no impact on the present.

Racial division remains a long-lived and deadly reality that desperately needs a prophetic word

---

[154] See Stephen R.C. Hicks, *Nietzsche and the Nazis* (Ockham's Razor Publishing, 2006), 40ff.

from God's people. Any prophetic response understands that, as Pope Paul VI noted, "If you want peace, work for justice."[155] As such, any answer to the question of how to respond to the problem of racism has to include justice. The problems of race cannot simply be whitewashed (pun intended), meaning they cannot be solved by demanding that people of color act white, unquestioningly follow white laws, and conform to white norms. That kind of reconciliation ignores the voices of people of color. It ignores justice. And so, it isn't reconciliation at all.

If white Christians truly want reconciliation, they are going to have to take seriously the voices of people of color. That means they are going to have to become educated about the racist history of "whiteness." White Christians will have to become students of people of color. The voices of modern-day prophets like James Cone, James Baldwin, Delores Williams, and myriad others need to be just as common to the church curriculum as the teachings of Moses and the Apostle Paul.

As radical as that may sound to some, it expresses the desperate need to apply the teachings of the Bible to contemporary societal problems. Peacemakers will have to be truly open to seeing and hearing the victims of oppression and

---

[155] See The Message of His Holiness Pope Paul VI for the Celebration of the Day of Peace, January 1, 1972.

understand the wisdom they bring to the table. *Solving the problems of race will never occur so long as white people uncritically view whiteness as an essential part of their identity.* We must be willing to examine critically the labels that history has thrust upon us. And, perhaps most importantly, we must be willing to be transformed by the renewing of our minds.[156]

---

[156] Romans 12:2.

Helping Samaritans

Jesus tells the story of a fellow Judean in desperate need of help.[157] Luke's original audience would have needed no explanation about how the Samaritans were the "bad guys." For hundreds of years, there had been a long-standing hatred between them and Judea. In the verses before Jesus' parable, the whole village of Samaritans had rejected Jesus outright.[158] What would he have to say about these people whom it would be so easy to dismiss?

As author and pastor Barbara Brown Taylor put it, "[Jews and Samaritans] had enough in common to disagree about who was right about God." She wrote, "They both claimed to possess the God-ordained scriptures, though not the same version. They both worshipped in a temple, though not the same one. They both claimed to be God's chosen people. Though neither would admit that God might have chosen more than one *chosen* people. Each group viewed the other as a bunch of vile imposters, unclean in the eyes of God." So, it was no surprise that a Samaritan would not welcome a Jew into his home, any more than a Jew would welcome a Samaritan.

---

[157] Luke 10:25–37. This section is an adaptation of a sermon titled *The Right Answer,* given by Barbara Brown Taylor at Riverside Church, New York NY, on July 16, 2013.

[158] Luke 9:51–56.

So deep was the disdain for one another that when Jesus was rejected in that Samaritan village, his disciples asked if they should rain down [hell fire] to burn those god-forsaken people to the ground.[159] Samaritans, they thought, were *that* irredeemable. In response, Jesus told them a story in which the irredeemable Samaritan was the hero, the godly neighbor, the merciful one.

Jesus flipped the script by placing a Samaritan in Jewish territory. Instead of the disciples feeling unwelcome, now the Samaritan finds hard times in Judea. In other words, Jesus turned everything they knew upside down when he put *good* and *Samaritan* together in the ears of his listeners for the very first time. Again, to quote Taylor, "[Jesus] knew that sometimes you have to start telling a different kind of story before a different kind of future can unfold."

If the story of the Good Samaritan doesn't make you cringe, then you haven't *really* heard the story. The whole point of it being a Samaritan is that Samaritans are the last people in the world that could be called good! That's how we know that we have lost this story's cutting edge, since the Samaritan in *our* culture is known, not as an enemy, but as a saint. So saintly, in fact, that we name hospitals and clinics and career centers and

---

[159] Luke 9:54.

relief agencies and educational institutions and nursing homes and even credit unions after him. The tension of the word "Good" beside the word "Samaritan" has been completely lost on us.

One author challenges us to try moving this whole story to the West Bank, "since that is where the ancient kingdom of Samaria was." If you want to feel the punch of the story, A. J. Levine noted, then imagine that the man in the ditch is one of your brothers or sisters in faith. Imagine someone you love beaten, robbed, half-naked, and left for dead. And then, after your pastor and then your bishop pass by without offering any help at all, imagine a Muslim member of Hamas bending down to bind your loved one's wounds, bathing them, and ensuring that they receive life-saving care.[160]

Levine's point is powerful, though probably for you and me it is not the West Bank we need to imagine. Where the story has to take place for *you*, only you know. Maybe it's down south at the Texas border. Those irredeemable illegals. Maybe it's at a Pride Rally. Those irredeemable transgenders. Maybe it's in North Carolina beneath a statue commemorating a Confederate soldier. Those irredeemable racists. Maybe it's at an alt-right fundraiser. Those irredeemable deplorables. Only *you* know where

---

[160] See Amy-Jill Levine's *Short Stories by Jesus* (New York: Harper One, 2015), 114, 115.

the story needs to take place so that *you* can truly hear it. Who is the last person in the world that you would want to have to tell everyone had saved your life? Who is the person that you would hate to admit was a blessing to you, an agent of God's care? *That* person is your "good" Samaritan.

As Taylor so poignantly noted, "The good news is only *good* once you have given up *your* ideas about who is good and who is bad." Of course, to hear Jesus tell it, the quickest way to give up *our* notions of who is good and who is bad is to get beaten up, and robbed, [and left for dead], because from that point of view, from the perspective of the ditch, *anyone at all* who stops to help—*that* is your experience of the presence of God in the world. That is your God-sighting. That is your "neighbor." In the Kingdom of God, your neighbor is *not* the person who looks the same as you, or the person who thinks like you do, or the person who worships like you do. Your neighbor is the one who is merciful to those who are most in need of mercy.

This, however, may lead us to something deeply troubling. And it is this: "Jesus does not care what the Samaritan believes. It's only what the man *does* that matters." Yes, his Holy Scriptures are different. Yes, he goes to a different temple. Yes, he claims a different religion. So what? Jesus's concern is for the man's actions. He isn't interested in his beliefs.

And, my goodness, this can be unsettling to Christians who have been taught that it is what we believe and not our works that matter most. But there it is! As Taylor put it, "[Jesus] was a Jew who knew that *right belief does not put a cup of water in the hands of a thirsty person, or bandage a wound, or offer a traveler a bed*. Right beliefs don't change a thing unless they lead to right actions."

Who are We in the Story?

One of the most uncomfortable commands of Jesus is to "Love your enemies."[161] What makes this scripture so uncomfortable is the strange realization that, as a white, heterosexual, cisgendered, able-bodied male, I do not experience a world filled with enemies. Don't get me wrong. I am acutely aware that, contrary to what my mother might believe, there are people who do not like me—at all! These people, however, are not my enemies. They aren't out to do me harm. Of course, I am told that I have enemies, and that the state and the military keep me safe from them. Maybe that's true; there is certainly evil in the world. But if I didn't hear it on the news, I wouldn't be aware of any particular person or people who actively seek to do me harm. On a personal and interpersonal level, I neither know nor encounter people in my daily life that I would call an enemy.

It is not trivial when we are unable to easily identify with the crowd to whom Jesus was preaching. The occupied people of Judea who were gathered around to hear Jesus's sermon would have had no problem understanding what Jesus meant by "enemies." They were surrounded by them. Far from ancient stories, daily life was marked by the realities of rulers (like King Herod) who had no

---

[161] Matthew 5:44.

qualms ordering the murder of all babies under the age of two, the powers-that-be arresting and executing prominent religious leaders like John the Baptist and Jesus, or (as Vespasian did) razing their temple, which was as much the center of political life as it was religious. Jesus' followers knew well what it meant to be always in the crosshairs, to always be on alert for abusers.

To the poor and hungry people living with real enemies, Jesus' words must have sounded impossible: "Love your enemies." Love those who force you into involuntary servitude without legal recourse. Love those who may maim or kill you or your loved ones with impunity. Love those who may put you in prison without just cause. It becomes unsettlingly clear that he was speaking to the disenfranchised and dehumanized. In other words, he wasn't speaking to people like me.

As an heir to the spoils of the genocide of Native Americans, brutal chattel slavery of African people, patriarchy silencing women's political voice, death-dealing policies that criminalized LGBTQIA persons, and dehumanization of those possessing neurodiversity, the reality is increasingly undeniable. *I am not the one called to love my enemies. I am the enemy to be loved.*

God's identity is found among "the least of these," even if we have a hard time locating our own identity there.[162] With whom we identify in the story is critical to our ability to understand it. Modern day benefactors of American's exploitative history are likely to have more in common with the Roman Empire than with the unfed masses who journeyed to hear Jesus preach sermons like "woe to the rich!" and "it is easier for a camel to pass through the eye of a needle than for a rich man to enter the kingdom of Heaven."[163]

Often, our psychological impulse is to tell ourselves that we are good. "All one's ways may be pure in one's own eyes, but the Lord weighs the spirit."[164] Scripture, on the other hand, commands God's people to "repent and believe the good news."[165] But what does it look like to repent? What are we to do?

---

[162] Matthew 25:40.

[163] Luke 6:24 and Matthew 19:24.

[164] Proverbs 16:2.

[165] Mark 1:15.

Charity and Justice

A church that appreciates Jubilee will understand the distinction between charity and justice. Charity is an indispensable aspect of Christian love. Giving generously to those in need is a command from Jesus himself. Feeding those who are hungry by working at a soup kitchen or donating to food pantries or clothing those who desperately need a coat or dry socks to survive cold winter nights while living under a bridge are life-saving blessings to those in need. As Martin Luther once wrote, "God doesn't need your good works, but your neighbor does."

Charity, however, has a dark side. James Cone claimed that, "Such acts are sin [or guilt] offerings that represent a white way of assuring themselves that they are basically a 'good' people.'"[166] Understanding that "whiteness" is tied to economies of superiority and subjugation, it becomes clearer that Cone is not talking about any particular white person, but about the economics of "whiteness" that is content to leave some languishing unto death while others enjoy abundance. Charity is a sin offering when it assuages guilt for participating in exploitative systems that leave children homeless or mothers

---

[166] See James Cone, *A Black Theology of Liberation* (Philadelphia, PA and New York: J.B. Lippincott Company, 1970), 124.

starving, or fathers imprisoned in an undeniably racialized justice system.[167]

Cone's point reminds the church that charity is an incomplete way of loving our neighbor. Dietrich Bonhoeffer is often attributed with saying, "If I sit next to a madman as he drives a car into a group of innocent bystanders, I can't, as a Christian, simply wait for the catastrophe [to end], then comfort the wounded and bury the dead. I must try to wrestle the steering wheel out of the hands of the driver." The story of the Dominican and Franciscan monks at the river provides a clear picture. Journeying together, they noticed a baby crying in terror floating down the river. "Quick," the Franciscan said, "let's grab the baby out of the water before it drowns." Soon, another baby, and then another, until a chain of babies came floating behind. While the Franciscan was scrambling frantically to save them all from a watery grave, the Dominican exclaimed, "I'm going upriver to see who's putting babies in the water!" Charity is pulling the infants out of the river. Justice is going upstream to put a stop to whoever is putting babies in mortal danger.

The problem with all of this was brilliantly stated by Brazilian Archbishop Dom Helder Camara. "If I give food to the poor, they call me a saint. When I

---

[167] See Richard Rothstein, *The Color of Law: A Forgotten History of How Our Government Segregated America* (New York, NY: Liveright Publishing Corporation, 2017).

ask why they are poor, they call me a communist." Camara's words typify how charitable works are often described as benevolent, while works of justice are seen as trouble.

Acts of charity like donating to local food banks are incredibly important. But they do nothing to challenge the political and economic systems that leave people in poverty. Acts of justice, on the other hand, are about changing systems and structures that create desperately hungry people. In other words, unlike doing charity, doing justice lands churches right in the middle of politics.

The idea that following Christ would land a church in the middle of politics should not be surprising. "Christ," after all, was not Jesus' last name. It was a title imbued with political significance. The Christ figure was prophesied in Hebrew scripture to rule in the line of King David, and, in the New Testament, to rule the world in the end. To turn Jesus into a spiritual king, while disallowing the politics of marginalized persons is to neuter the meaning of the word "Christ." To proclaim Christ as King is deeply political.

One of the things that makes politics so troubling is the fact that it involves choosing sides. That, however, has never been a problem for liberation theologians like Gustavo Gutiérrez. Reading scripture, one quickly gets the impression that ***God is a God who takes sides!*** To hear the story of

Pharaoh and his army drowning in the river as the slaves escaped is to recognize immediately that the biblical God is not afraid to choose one people over another. And the side that God takes, Gutierrez insists, is the side of the poor.[168] "In Jesus Christ, God has demonstrated God's preferential option for the poor."

The claim that "Black Lives Matter" is not altogether unsimilar to the proclamation that "God is on the side of the poor." Both of these proclamations come out of histories of exploitation. The common responses that "All lives matter" or that "God loves everyone" are mired in deafness and denial, because they fail to recognize suffering and injustice. They represent a refusal either to look or to listen to the cry of God's people.

Jubilee is an act of liberation and restoration for the oppressed, not only from slavery and its lasting legacy, but also for those suffering the death-dealing effects of oppression. This lands the church in the midst of politics because oppressions become systemic through political policies. To help the poor includes addressing the structures and systems that allow crushing poverty to flourish. Changing this system is exactly what Leviticus 25 was about;

---

[168] See Gustavo Gutierrez and Cardinal Gerhar Ludwig Muller, *On the Side of the Poor: The Theology of Liberatio*n. Orbis Books (March 10, 2015)

namely, putting legal policies in place that alleviate human suffering.

Poverty and race are only a beginning. Oppression has many faces: gender, age, sexual orientation, religious, mental and physical ability, and more. To enact a Jubilee gospel means that churches engage in the political arena to amplify the voices of the voiceless, and to work on behalf of justice. "For the Spirit of the Lord is upon me, because he has anointed me to proclaim good news to the poor. He has sent me to proclaim liberty to the captives . . . and to set at liberty those who are oppressed."[169]

---

[169] Luke 4:18.

An Imagination for the Impossible

To proclaim such a hope does not come easy. In fact, it borders on naïve. Much of what passes for Christianity seems more self-serving than world-saving. Churches today seem no more willing to proclaim and enact a Jubilee gospel than in times past. In fact, just the opposite. Televangelists and prosperity gospel preachers fill sports stadiums proclaiming a message of *personal* salvation and wealth creation.

Scripture, however, has a way of being honest about the difficulties of discipleship, where doubt seems an ever-present companion. The disciple Thomas modeled doubt perfectly when he said, "Until I see the nail holes in his hands, and put my fingers in the nail holes . . . I will not believe."[170] One of the most fascinating verses of that story is that even with the resurrected Jesus right in front of them, they were still filled with doubts. As Luke put it, "While in their joy, they were disbelieving."[171] Another favorite example of doubt is when Jesus was giving the Great Commission in Matthew to go and make disciples of all nations. He gave that Great Commission to a group of doubting disciples.[172] Were they doubting resurrection? Or,

---

[170] John 20:25.

[171] Luke 24:41.

[172] Matthew 28:17.

after witnessing the arrest, beating, and murder of Jesus, were they doubting that anything like God's Kingdom could ever come to fruition?

In fact, all of the Gospel accounts have doubt stories. All of them! Doubt stories are found so often in scripture that doubting just might make you disciple-of-Jesus material. At the very least, doubt is just as much a part of the resurrection story as is faith.

And maybe we could just leave it at that. Your doubt is enough to qualify you as disciple material. Just ask Matthew and Mark and Luke and John and good ol' Doubting Thomas. As much as the disciples of old, your doubt is welcome. Your doubt is in the company of sacred scripture.

But if we did just leave it at that, we might miss something beautiful about biblical doubt. And there *is* something beautiful about the unbelievability of the resurrection. This foundational event of faith, Easter itself, creates a unique imagination. It invites us to think differently about what others may call "unbelievable;" and to see more clearly what others may deem absurd. The Church has been gifted a beautiful imagination for the impossible.

Sometimes there are glaring examples of this beautiful Easter imagination. The Reverend Dr. Martin Luther King, Jr.'s imagination for the impossible stirred a hope for racial equality like the world had never seen. Such imagination is a threat to the powers and principalities of this world. It is a threat to imagine that things don't have to be the way that they are. But imagining such impossible things is a gift for those who suffer injustice; it is a gift for those who long for the promises of God. People capable of imagining the impossible are a dangerous people because they bring hope where there would otherwise be no reason to hope.

Imagination for the impossible belongs to each and every one of us when we hold firmly, with faith and with doubt, to the ridiculous idea that the dead are raised;[173] the outlandish belief that the meek will inherit the earth;[174] and the irrational conviction that the weakness of the cross is more powerful than the forces of brutality and violence.[175] Those who hold firmly with faith in such doubtable things are able to see the beautiful in the unbelievable.

The Church is an Easter people who can see the impossible for what it is—the power of hope in the midst of doubt; the vision to see a brand-new thing; the power to see life where death seems to reign. *To say that resurrection is unbelievable does not*

---

[173] Luke 20:37.

[174] Matthew 5:5.

[175] 1 Corinthians 1:25. Here, "human strength" is in context to the power of the cross as an implement of terror and control.

strip it of its power. To say that resurrection is unbelievable is to name its power. Resurrection is only the beginning of the impossible things the Church believes. It believes, also, that love conquers hate. It believes that forgiveness is more powerful than vengeance. It believes that grace and not merit makes a person worthy of love. The Church is a people whose spiritual practice deepens their imagination for all the unbelievable things that "God has prepared for those who love him."[176]

---

[176] 1 Corinthians 2:9.

Chapter 10:
PROCLAIMING A JUBILEE GOSPEL

By Whose Authority?

The Gospel of Mark recounts a time when Jesus entered the Temple courts. While teaching, some of the elders, scribes, and chief priests came to him and asked, "By what authority are you doing these things?"[177] By what authority does one speak about God's activity in the world? Interestingly, Jesus didn't answer the question. What he did instead was expose the ways such questions reflect the human ego. The elders, chief priests, and scribes were the subject matter experts. How dare anyone else imagine they could speak with authority about what God is up to!

Experiencing God's life-saving word in times of overwhelming pain indelibly shapes one's faith. Meaningful theology flows from one's experience of the divine. To share the painful stories of life— stories of vulnerability—is to share the depths from

---

[177] Mark 11:28ff.

which one has been rescued. Like the deaf and mute man that Jesus healed, then "ordered... not to tell anyone," "the more [Jesus told him not to tell], the more he kept talking about it."[178] The man born deaf and mute couldn't help but share the ways in which he experienced the life-changing event of God. What began as a story of pain became a divine encounter that set his life on a new trajectory filled with hope and promise.

Right along with the pathos of the Hebrew people, the good news is expressed in the laws, the historical memory, and in the hope for their future. From the beginning, the Gospel is a message of good news for those who know what it feels like to be abandoned, taken advantage of, brutalized, and subjugated.

Professor of theology Douglass John Hall, in his work *Why Christian: For Those on the Edge of Faith*, pulled no punches about how off put by Jesus most would be today. No respectable middle-class family, Hall insisted, would ever want their child to grow up to be like Jesus! "For all intents and purposes, he was a loser. Dead at thirty-something, rejected by nearly everybody, even his followers, crying out in pain and loneliness from his cross."[179]

---

[178] Mark 7:36.
[179] See Douglas John Hall, *Why Christian? For Those on the Edge of Faith* (Minneapolis, MN: Fortress Press, 1998), 17.

What gives one "ears to hear" is not the academic degree they hold or prestigious office they fill. What gives them "ears to hear" is the life they've lived, which is why not everyone heard *good news* when Jesus proclaimed the gospel.

Just who heard the gospel as good news? Clearly, not the powerful. They had Jesus killed. Not the religious elites. They called him the spawn of Satan.[180] Not the rich. They went away dejected and sad.[181] The ones who heard the proclamation as *good news* were the sick and outcast and poor and brokenhearted.

One of the most instructive stories of Jesus is *The Parable of the Talents*. There was a nobleman who had to leave town on business, and he left three slaves in charge. To one, he gave five talents. To another, two talents. And to the last, only one. Returning, he called his slaves to see what profits they had earned in his absence. The first slave proudly said, "Master, you handed over to me five talents, and I have made five talents more." The nobleman was thrilled to receive one hundred percent earnings. "Well done, good and faithful servant," he exclaimed. Similarly, the second slave with the two talents made two more. "Well done, good and faithful servant," the master said. But the

---

[180] Luke 11:15.

[181] Luke 12:13–21.

third slave, handing back the one talent, said this: "Master, I knew that you were a harsh man, reaping where you do not sow, and gathering where you did not scatter seed; so, I was afraid, and I went and hid your talent in the ground. Here, take back what is yours."[182]

In a First World context, it is not uncommon to hear this parable as a message about the value of hard work. "Well done, good and faithful servant. You have been trustworthy in a few things. I will put you in charge of many things." In a culture that upholds the axiom that "hard work equals success," this interpretation fits well into already existing assumptions. Work hard, get rewarded! Do as the third slave did, and you would certainly hear, "You wicked and lazy servant!"[183]

Ched Myers noticed the First World tendency to "thoroughly domesticate the parable under *our* status quo. Stories meant to challenge our preconceptions are thus used to legitimate them."[184] His point was that most of us hear the parable of the talents as a story that congratulates hard work and profit-making.

---

[182] Matthew 25:14–30.

[183] Matthew 25:26ff.

[184] See Ched Myers, *The Biblical Vision of Sabbath Economics*, The Church of the Saviour, Washington DC, 2001, p. 39.

Far from glorifying those who worked hard and earned profit, Myers continued, the slave who buried the coin in the ground was the true hero of the parable. This is a parable about holy non-participation in evil. In an act of brave defiance, the slave refused to participate in a system in which one "reaps where they did not sow and harvests where they did not scatter seed."

In fact, part of what makes this defiance so *brave* is the punishment that the slave received. You cannot defy the powers-that-be in this world and not feel the consequences. If we first imagine that the punishment is a description of Hell, we aren't far from the truth. In a world that invented the lynching tree for those who sought escape from power's cruelty and injustice, the cross must feel exactly like a living hell. Those who fail to participate in their own exploitation—and not only that, but then have the audacity to call out the sin of "harvesting where you did not sow" and "gathering where you did not scatter seed"—they know exactly what it means to be "[thrown] into the outer darkness, where there will be weeping and gnashing of teeth."[185] This outer darkness is not a metaphor for eternal damnation. It is a metaphor for what happens when you refuse to go along with your oppressors.

---

185 Matthew 25:29–30.

While First World interpretations often imagine the nobleman as the god-figure, *would Jesus tell a parable characterizing God as a harsh master who profits from unjust means?* Rather than hearing the parable as *prescriptive*, Myers interprets the story as descriptive. "The original audience of this story would not have had to allegorize to make sense of it."[186] In other words, Jesus is describing what it looks like to be a disciple in a world in which the powerful use brutality to maintain the status quo. Jesus doesn't pretend that defying the powers-that-be will make you popular or financially well off. Anyone who bucks the system in *this* world of greed and violence will suffer the consequences. *The Parable of the Talents* assumes the Jubilee promise that God is on the side of the exploited.

---

[186] See Ched Myers' *The Biblical Vision of Sabbath Economics*, The Church of the Saviour, Washington DC, 2001, page 41.

Everything You Need

It helps to remember that Jesus' teachings were not new. Even when he used the language of "A new commandment I give you, to love one another," (John 13:34) he was quoting Leviticus 19:18. In fact, the Gospel of Matthew works hard to present Jesus as the new Moses. Giving a sermon "on the mount" in a place where no mountains existed is a great clue to this.

Using unmistakable symbolism, Matthew wanted his readers to think of Jesus as the new Moses. "You have heard it said, 'an eye for an eye.'" "You have heard it said, 'you shall not commit adultery.'" "You have heard it said, 'you shall not murder.'" Jesus was clear that he "did not come to abolish the [Old Testament] law, but to fulfill it."[187] The Gospels go a long way to make connections between the good news found in the Hebrew Bible and the good news proclaimed in the New Testament.

And that gospel is clearly proclaimed in Isaiah 61. "The Lord has anointed me to bring good news to the *oppressed*, to bind up the *brokenhearted*, to proclaim liberty to the *captives*, and release to the *prisoners*, to proclaim the year of the Lord's favor." Early Jewish, Talmudic literature was quick to make connections between "the Year of the Lord's

---

[187] Matthew 5:17.

Favor" in Isaiah 61 and "the Year of Jubilee" in Leviticus 25. The Gospel has always (even in the Hebrew Bible) been God's response to suffering, to oppression, to broken heartedness, and to all the ways we are made captive.

Our personal stories of heartbreak are not trivial. Rather, they are powerful. The Gospel in both testaments is that your pain matters deeply to God. Your shouts of heartbreak are heard. "The Lord said, 'I have indeed seen the misery of my people… and I am aware of their sufferings.'"[188] Scripture's response to our heartbreak is the Gospel—the good news. God is at work on behalf of all those who know injustice and heartache. And everyone who has encountered that divine word of hope and healing has everything they need to share the message.

---

[188] Exodus 3:7.

Made in the USA
Coppell, TX
08 April 2022

76257309R10094